CW00551588

# THE JOSHUA DELUSION?

# THE JOSHUA DELUSION?

## Rethinking Genocide in the Bible

Douglas Earl

CASCADE *Books* • Eugene, Oregon

THE JOSHUA DELUSION?
Rethinking Genocide in the Bible

Copyright © 2010 Douglas Earl. All rights reserved. Except for brief quotations in critical publications or reviews, no part of this book may be reproduced in any manner without prior writeen permission from the publisher. Write: Permissions, Wipf and Stock Publishers, 199 W. 8th Ave., Suite 3, Eugene, OR 97401.

Cascade Books
An imprint of Wipf and Stock Publishers
199 W. 8th Ave., Suite 3
Eugene, OR 97401

www.wipfandstock.com

ISBN 13: 978-1-60899-892-0

Cataloguing-in-Publication data

---

Earl, Douglas

The Joshua Delusion?: rethinking genocide in the Bible/Douglas Earl

xvi+174 pp.; 22 cm. Includes bibliographical references.

ISBN 13: 978-1-60899-892-0

1. Bible. O.T. Joshua—Criticism, interpretation, etc., 2. War—Biblical teaching. 3. Violence in the Bible. I. Title.

BS1295.52 E27 2010

---

Manufactured in the U.S.A.

For Rachel

# Contents

# Preface

This book has emerged out of my concern to understand what it means to read the Bible well as an evangelical Christian who wishes to take the implications of historical and ethical difficulties in the Bible with full seriousness in the context of 'faith seeking understanding'. The book is based upon my PhD thesis, 'Reading Joshua as Christian Scripture' submitted to Durham University in 2008. The initial spur to write this thesis came from a research seminar on the book of Judges at Spurgeon's College in 2004. At the seminar it seemed to me that there was a general mood of wanting to claim all the Old Testament as Christian Scripture, but that the books of Joshua and Judges in particular seemed to present a serious obstacle to this. Shortly after this at Durham University I wrote an essay for an MA module on the theological interpretation of Scripture that addressed the question of how theological interpretation of Scripture might be formulated and practised in the face of criticisms that it is likely either to entail bad history or to be ideologically manipulative (or both). In this essay I considered Joshua very briefly in the light of historical and ethical difficulties with the book, but I was not really satisfied with what I had done here. These concerns led to the three year research project which forms the basis of this book, a project funded by the Arts and Humanities Research Council, whose funding I am most grateful for.

This book is, therefore, the result of a long and sometimes difficult journey, a journey which has been guided and shaped by a number of people to whom I owe much gratitude. First

x *Preface*

and foremost, my PhD supervisor, Prof R.W.L. Moberly has been instrumental in guiding this journey and shaping this work. I have also benefited greatly from time spent with others in conversations about my work, especially with regard to the use of contemporary anthropological work. In particular I would like to express my thanks to Prof Douglas Davies for helping find my bearings in the interface between the domains of anthropology and theology, to Prof Robert Segal for helping me to get to grips with myth, and to Prof Seth Kunin for introducing me to neo-structuralism. But many others at Durham, both staff and students, have helped to shape my thinking for this book, especially Dr Chris Insole, Dr Marcus Pound and Dr Stuart Weeks. Prior to arriving at Durham Dr John Colwell, Dr Martin Selman and Dr Stephen Wright at Spurgeon's College, and Dr Stephen Dray and Steve King at Moorlands College were all instrumental in preparing me for what has ended up as this book. Outside the academic context over these many years the fellowship of the Sutcliff Baptist Church in Olney has provided much spiritual, pastoral and practical help for which I and my family are most grateful.

Turning to the book itself, I am indebted to Dr Robin Parry for commissioning the work and for his suggestions for improvements to the text, and to Dr Chris Wright for writing a response to it. I would also like to thank Dr Richard Briggs, David Childs and Valerie Hornsby for their helpful comments on a draft of this book, and to Dr Murray Rae at Eisenbrauns for allowing me to write a more popular level version of my PhD thesis which Eisenbrauns are publishing (in slightly revised form) as Reading Joshua as Christian Scripture.

Finally, as always my family has provided vital support and encouragement in seeing this work through to completion, and so I must express my gratitude to Rachel my wife and my children Sophie, Daniel, Sarah, Peter, Hannah and Matthew.

# Foreword

Evangelical Christians are characterized by, among other things, high regard, indeed reverence, for Scripture. The Bible is the word of God. This means, among other things, that the Bible is understood to contain the self-revelation of the one true God, who is made known in many and various ways, and supremely in Jesus Christ. As such, the Bible is to be trusted and what it says is to be carried out – this is the way to live life most fully and faithfully.

Unfortunately, there are many difficulties within the Bible. Sometimes it is a problem of understanding what the text is saying. But even more problematic is when we think we do understand what the text is saying, but what it appears to be saying makes the heart sink. This may be because of the costliness of the challenge to faithfulness. But often, especially in the Old Testament, it is because the content may appear to be at odds with Christian priorities. What should one do, for example, with the imprecatory psalms, when the New Testament directs that Christians should bless, and not curse, those who persecute them?

At present, the relationship between faith in God and violence towards those considered to be others/outsiders is a live issue, nurtured not least by the indiscriminate murder of people in their normal course of life by Islamist suicide bombers. To be sure, one of the striking things about Jesus's death and resurrection, which Christians hold at the heart of their faith, is that it is at nobody's expense: the only one who suffers and dies is Jesus himself, and the risen Jesus offers life even to those who put him to death. However, although this is at the heart of Scripture, it has to be recognized that not everything in Scripture straightforwardly conforms to this pattern. Especially in the Old Testament, it is clear, for example, that Israel is given a land to live in at the expense of its former inhabitants, the Canaanites.

Difficulties about religiously-inspired violence, and God's favour for some being at the expense of depriving others, come together with unusual force in the book of Joshua. This book can appear to be an account of divinely-sponsored ethnic cleansing. As such, it not only offers ammunition to those hostile to Christian faith; but also for evangelical Christians, who are committed to a reverential and trusting attitude towards Scripture, it can be unclear how best to handle such a text. This difficulty is not, of course, a new one, but it is perhaps particularly pressing at the present time. In recent scholarship this moral and theological difficulty has also been supplemented by another difficulty as to the historicity of Joshua's account of the conquest, not least because the archaeological evidence poses problems.

How should all these difficulties be handled well? Generally speaking, the more something matters, the harder it can be to discuss it carefully and dispassionately – heated rhetoric, partisan arguments, unexamined assumptions, defensiveness, and point-scoring all too easily accompany, and often displace, searching engagement with the real issues.

I am delighted, therefore, to commend this book as a model of how to approach difficulties in Scripture. Douglas Earl offers a way of thinking about Joshua that will be surprising and challenging to many. Yet, whether or not his thesis fully persuades, the way in which he approaches the text will surely appeal to all thoughtful Christians; for Earl is simultaneously radical, in that he utilizes fresh resources and challenges common ways of thinking about Joshua, and traditional, in that he reconnects with certain ancient and existentially fruitful Christian ways of handling the text. Moreover, the response from Chris Wright, and Earl's reply to this response, model respectful and attentive scholarly interaction and the shared quest of faith seeking understanding. Tolle, lege – take up, and read.

*Walter Moberly, Abbey House, Palace Green, Durham, UK.*

# Introduction

It would be interesting to conduct an opinion poll of Christians in order to discover what the biggest obstacle to delving into the Old Testament is today. For some it might be the detailed laws; for others it might be the repetitive histories and genealogies, or it might be the alien or perhaps seemingly irrelevant world that is presented there. But I suspect that for many the problem is often that of pictures of genocide and violence, especially now that we are all too familiar with harrowing scenes of violence and its aftermath on our TV screens. How is this violent world of the Old Testament, a world of violence in which both the people of God and God seem implicated, in any way compatible with the world of the gospels, with the kingdom of God, and with a God of love?

Sadly, we have become all too familiar with religiously motivated terror attacks in the name of 'holy war' and genocides in the name of 'ethnic cleansing'. In many ways the questions posed to us by some, such as Richard Dawkins in particular, are unsurprising and fair. In light of various religiously motivated terror attacks and genocides, and in light of reading the Bible, is religion simply a stimulus for violence and evil – the ultimate delusion? Or, even if one does not wish to go so far as Dawkins, might Christians now wish to abandon the Old Testament altogether as it seems to reflect a del-uded view of a violent God, a view of God that seemingly led to genocide and violence in ancient times?

As Christians we need to face the problem head on. There is no denying that there are a number of stories steeped in

'genocide' (to use a specific modern term that does not necessarily correspond with what we find in the Bible) in the Old
Testament.1 Turning to Genesis, the very first book of the Old
Testament, in Genesis 34 we find a story of rape, deception and
the massacre of the Shechemites by Jacob's sons. Turning to
Exodus, the next book in the Bible, we find an account of the
war against the Amalekites (Exodus 17) which concludes with
the report that God will blot out the memory of Amalek (Exod.
17:14). And in Numbers, the fourth book, there are several
massacres reported and indeed condoned (Num 21:1–3, 21–35;
25). But perhaps it is in the following books of Deuteronomy
and Joshua that we find the most comprehensive and difficult
accounts of dispossession of peoples, genocide and destruction in the Old Testament. In Deuteronomy 7 Israel is commanded to 'utterly destroy' the local inhabitants of the land
together with all their idols and altars (7:1–5). The book of
Joshua reports the fulfilment of this campaign of destruction
and the settlement of Israel in the land, being a book filled with
reports of genocide and destruction. Reading past Joshua we
come straight to the bloody history of the book of Judges, and
then in the books of Samuel and Kings we have accounts of
warfare and violence abounding. On the whole these accounts
in Samuel and Kings seem more concerned with warfare in
general rather than with genocide and conquest on the part of
Israel, perhaps with 1 Samuel 15, where Saul is commanded to
'utterly destroy' the Amalekites, being the main exception.

The term used in the original Hebrew texts for this 'utter
destruction' in 1 Samuel 15, Deuteronomy 7 and Joshua is the
word herem.2 It is a rather rare word outside Deuteronomy
and Joshua, yet perhaps it captures the essence of the problem
of genocide in the Bible. So this idea of herem sums up for us
in the sharpest way what is problematic in the Old Testament
with regard to the problems of violence and genocide in the
name of God, and I think that it is fair to say that it is the book
of Joshua that provides the most comprehensive treatment of
the idea of herem in the Old Testament. Indeed, in his book
The God Delusion Richard Dawkins singles out the narrative
of Joshua together with the commands of Deuteronomy suggesting that:

The ethnic cleansing begun in the time of Moses is brought to bloody fruition in the book of Joshua, a text remarkable for the bloodthirsty massacres it records and the xenophobic relish with which it does so. As the charming old song exultantly has it, 'Joshua fit the battle of Jericho, and the walls came a-tumbling down . . . There's none like good old Joshuay, at the battle of Jericho.' Good old Joshua didn't rest until 'they utterly destroyed all that was in the city, both man and woman, young and old, and ox, and sheep, and ass, with the edge of the sword' (Joshua 6:21) . . . Do not think, by the way, that the God character in the story nursed any doubts or scruples about the massacres and genocides that accompanied the seizing of the Promised Land. On the contrary, his orders, for example in Deuteronomy 20, were ruthlessly explicit.[3]

For these reasons I would like to focus attention in this book on the problem of genocide as we find it in Joshua – it seems to be the most obvious and troublesome example of the problem. So what I would like to do is to consider what the book of Joshua is about, as a book that was significant for ancient Israel, the church through the ages, and for Christians today. What is the real significance of the book? Is it a book glorifying in genocide and 'ethnic cleansing' – or is there in fact something much more subtle going on? I propose that there is in fact something more subtle going on in the book, and I shall try and develop and demonstrate this as we go along.

So, in chapter 1 I shall survey the origins of both the problems that the book of Joshua has raised for Christians, and the roots of possible ways of reading it that might point to a different way of understanding the book. This chapter offers a very brief summary of some Christian approaches to reading more problematic texts in the Old Testament. In chapter 2 I turn to look at some recent approaches to literature and narrative, especially from the perspective of anthropological analysis, to consider how important (but often difficult) stories function in shaping the lives of communities generally. Here I try to show that such an approach can be used to shed light on much traditional Christian reading of the Old Testament, and how an anthropologically guided approach might be a helpful

resource for us today as Christian readers of the Old
Testament. Chapter 2 is, perhaps, the most technically difficult
chapter of the book, but there is important material here that
lays the groundwork for the approach to Joshua that I take. In
chapter 3 I take a look at some of the important background
ideas for reading Joshua, especially a consideration of the idea
of herem and the nature of 'conquest accounts' in the ancient
Near Eastern world. Then in chapter 4 I develop a reading of
Joshua, trying to show what it is basically about and how it
might have been significant for the ancient Israelite; and in
chapter 5 I consider what significance Joshua might then have
in a Christian context, allowing for both continuity and discontinuity with its context in the Old Testament. Finally in
chapter 6 I discuss the implications of my reading of Joshua
more generally, making some brief remarks on how this might
relate to other texts in the Old Testament that portray genocide, as well as giving brief consideration to the implications
that this study has for our interpretation and use of the Old
Testament more generally.

With this in mind, it is worth reading through the book of
Joshua, and Deuteronomy 7, to familiarize yourself with the
material before going further. I have tried to leave out as much
of the technical detail as possible. For those who want more
detail, please consult my *Reading Joshua as Christian Scripture*
(Winona Lake: Eisenbrauns, forthcoming) where full details of
the arguments and discussions are supplied. In terms of commentaries on the text of Joshua, I have found L.D. Hawk's
commentary in the Berit Olam series most helpful for a literary
reading of Joshua, and I have drawn upon it regu-larly. For a
recent discussion of the more historical-critical issues involved
in reading Joshua R.D. Nelson's commentary is very useful,
and for an overview of traditional reading of Joshua the
Ancient Christian Commentary on Scripture (*Old Testament IV*)
by J.R. Franke is good.

# 1.

# If Jericho was Razed, is our Faith in Vain?

> So Joshua defeated the whole land . . . he left no one remaining,
> but utterly destroyed all that breathed, as the LORD God of
> Israel commanded. (Josh. 10:40, NRSV)

## Facing the historical problem: If Jericho was *not* razed, is our faith in vain?

In his 1982 book, *The Quest for the Historical Israel: Reconstructing Israel's Early History*, G.W. Ramsey devotes a chapter to the question, 'If Jericho was not Razed, is our Faith in Vain?'[1] The question is a witty allusion to 1 Corinthians 15:14 (if Christ has not been raised, then . . . your faith has been in vain). Ramsey asks the question in order to consider how the 'historical truth' of an Old Testament narrative affects its theological value. In other words, if Jericho was not utterly destroyed as described in Joshua 6, then does the story lack truth and theological value? Does a history-like narrative have to describe accurately events that have 'happened' for it to be 'true' and thus theologically valuable? Written in 1982, Ramsey's book emerged at about the time when 'literary' approaches to Old Testament narratives were becoming popular, approaches that began to make concerns with the question of what actually happened seem less important – it was what the story taught, as a story, that was coming to be seen as what was theologically significant. Theologically speaking, this kind of approach to the Bible might be said to reflect the coming of age of the ground-breaking work of Karl Barth earlier in the twentieth century. Barth argued that to become fixed on historical questions, with the actual events that may or may not be *behind* the story, could be unhelpful in terms of faithfully reading Scripture, suggesting that

> the idea that the Bible declares the Word of God only when it speaks historically is one which must be abandoned, especially in the Christian Church. One consequence of this misunderstanding was the great uncertainty of faith which resulted from an inability wholly to escape the impression that many elements in the Bible have the nature of saga, and an ignorance of where and how to draw the line which marks off what is finally historical and therefore the true Word of God. But in other cases it led to a rigid affirmation that in the Bible, as the Word of God, we have only 'historical' accounts and no saga at all – an affirmation which can be sustained only it we either close our eyes or violently reinterpret what we see. In other cases again it resulted in an attempt to penetrate to a 'historical' kernel which is supposed to give us the true, i.e., 'historical' word of God – the only trouble being that in the process it was unfortunately found that with the discarding of saga we do lose not only a subsidiary theme but the main point at issue, i.e., the biblical witness. We have to realise that in all three cases the presumed equation of the Word of God with a 'historical' record is an inadmissible postulate which does not itself originate in the Bible at all but in the unfortunate habit of Western thought which assumes that the reality of a history stands or falls by whether it is 'history.'[2]

In other words, by concentrating too much on questions of history we start to lose sight of the Bible itself and what it wishes to teach us.

However, the force of Ramsey's question with regard to the book of Joshua was acute in the twentieth century. Indeed, the historical difficulties that gradually emerged with Joshua may well have gone beyond what Barth envisaged, for in the early twentieth century the German Old Testament scholar Albrecht Alt argued that there never was an Israelite conquest of Canaan. But perhaps more famously the results of Dame Kathleen Kenyon's archaeological research on Jericho in the 1950s suggested that Jericho's walls had not fallen in an era that would correspond with the biblical record of its conquest by Israel. Hence Ramsey's question, for in the twentieth century many Christians were brought up in a context where 'history' was prized over against 'fiction' or 'myth', where what was 'historical' was 'truthful' whilst what was 'fictional' was 'false', and what was 'mythical' was regarded as naïve and untrue. So many Christians would naturally be worried that their faith may be in vain if indeed Jericho had not been razed – for the Bible's 'truth' seems to be eroded if it is not historically accurate. However, whilst today many, and perhaps most Old Testament scholars would probably assume that Israel did not conquer Canaan and settle in the land in the way that the book of Joshua presents it, several scholars have run against the tide and argued for another look at the archaeological data, scholars such as John Bimson and Peter James.[3] If their work is along the right lines, it might be possible to suggest that Jericho was indeed razed by the Israelites. And then the 'crisis of faith' can be averted – or can it?

## Facing the ethical problem: If Jericho was razed is our faith in vain?

The first problem is of course that even if archaeological evidence could prove that the Israelites did indeed raze Jericho then it in no way verifies the interpretation of the event given in the book of Joshua unless one makes the prior assumption that what the Bible describes is always automatically true. So in an 'apologetic' context (i.e., one in which one is seeking to provide evidence for the reliability of the Bible and its portrait of God, so as to convince others of this) one cannot claim for certain that God did indeed command the razing of Jericho. Archaeologically 'proving' that a group of Israelites razed

Jericho does not prove that God told them to or that the story that Joshua tells interprets events such as this correctly. But even if Joshua can be placed on a more 'historical' footing, there is a second problem – the ethical problem. The rise of ethical and postcolonial criticism of the biblical texts coupled with a raised global awareness of the horrors of religiously motivated violence and genocide in the late twentieth and early twenty-first centuries makes Joshua profoundly troubling reading.[4]

So, even if one could assert the historical value of Joshua after all, whilst this may well be of comfort to some Christians, it merely raises new ethical problems for others. For many Christians the ethical difficulties with the Old Testament are far more pressing than historical difficulties. So perhaps the problem now in the twenty-first century is the opposite of that which Ramsey posed in 1982. In other words for us the question is, 'If Jericho *was* razed, is our faith in vain?' Do we want to worship a cruel, violent and brutal God, particularly where religiously motivated violence is one of the biggest problems facing the contemporary world?

## The Joshua Delusion?

Posing the question in this way with these concerns has lead to a new kind of Christian apologetic along the following lines: we now believe that there was no conquest (according to mainstream archaeology) and so everything is OK as God is not violent and brutal after all – Israel just had an incorrect understanding of God. So the problem is shifted to a primitive and deluded concept of God in the minds of Ancient Israelites, exemplified by Joshua – the 'Joshua delusion' perhaps.

However, R.A. Warrior has drawn attention to the problem with this sort of apologetic appeal to history behind the text. He suggests that whatever the answer to the historical question of what history lies behind the text, it does not resolve the problem of the narrative. People read stories as they are, perhaps as a basis for political action, and not the history behind them.[5] Indeed, Richard Dawkins suggests

Yet again, theologians will protest, it [the fall of Jericho as per Joshua 6] didn't happen. Well, no – the story has it that the walls came tumbling down at the mere sound of men shouting and blowing horns, so indeed it didn't happen – but that is not the point. The point is that, whether true or not, the Bible is held up to us as the source of our morality. And the Bible story of Joshua's destruction of Jericho, and the invasion of the Promised Land in general, is morally indistinguishable from Hitler's invasion of Poland, or Saddam Hussein's massacres of the Kurds and the Marsh Arabs. The Bible may be an arresting and poetic work of fiction, but it is not the sort of book you should give your children to form their morals.[6]

With what I have termed the 'new apologetic' approach it is not the biblical text that is important, but what we think did or did not happen in the past behind the text that is important. But this approach represents a reversal of Barth's suggestion, and the comments of Warrior and Dawkins draw attention to the problems of this approach: Where does such an apologetic approach leave the biblical *text* itself? Remember that it is the text that the church has accepted as authoritative and *not the history behind the text*. So does the text of Joshua itself have any positive theological value – or is it an embarrassing hindrance to proclaiming the gospel today in a world torn apart by religiously motivated violence?

In a 'post-colonial' reading of Joshua Dora Mbuwayesango concludes that

> the book of Joshua can help the people of God to construct its identity in a sound way, namely by acknowledging and making explicit the revulsion we have for its narratives. Precisely because these stories of relentless massacres shock us, they warn us that the construction of identities that are exclusive and religiously sanctioned – however overt or covert this religious exclusivism might be – leads to genocide and extermination of entire ethnic groups.[7]

In other words, for Mbuwayesango, we should invert the way that the book of Joshua is used today. The text becomes a warning, and offers a viewpoint to be firmly rejected rather than followed.

But is there something else that might be said about Joshua? According to some of those concerned with the moral use of the Bible today and throughout the history of the Church the answer would seem to be a firm 'No'. It is claimed that the story of Joshua has been used historically to justify violence. For instance, Warrior indicates the problematic nature of conquest narratives in the Old Testament, and Joshua in particular, and highlights the use made of extracts from such narratives by Puritan emigrants to America to support genocide,[8] illustrating the point that Dawkins and Warrior himself makes above. Dawkins' (and Warrior's) point is illustrated again in the Crusades according to Roland Bainton – the narrative of Joshua, or so it is alleged, shaped the morals and actions of the crusaders. In his influential work, *Christian Attitudes to War and Peace*, Bainton titles a chapter 'The Origins of the Crusading Idea in the Old Testament', and discusses texts from Deuteronomy and Joshua, as well as other accounts of what he terms 'crusading' in the Old Testament.[9] As the title of the chapter suggests, he links the narrative of Joshua to the idea of 'crusade', repeatedly using the category of 'crusade' in relation to this and other Old Testament narratives. He concludes this chapter by stating, 'The architects of the Christian crusade, therefore, drew their warrant from the books of the conquest and of the Maccabean revolt.'[10]

Whilst Bainton wrote before the rise of colonial and post-colonial studies, his work has been used in the development of these fields of study in relation to the Bible. For example, Michael Prior argues for a moral critique of the Bible and its use in colonialism. Whilst he does not discuss the Crusades at length, he discusses Joshua and the Old Testament alongside the Crusades,[11] and suggests that the 'Crusades provide a striking example of the link between religious and political power, and exemplify how the Bible has been employed as an agent of oppression'.

In light of these comments and the all too frequent images of religiously motivated violence that we see on our TV screens there would seem to be little that one might intelligently say in response. For many, Calvin's reading of Joshua 10:18 seems rather hollow, and indeed closer to the problem than to a solution:

> The enemy having been completely routed, Joshua is now free, as it were, at leisure, to inflict punishment on the kings. In considering this, the divine command must always be kept in view. But for this it would argue boundless arrogance and barbarous atrocity to trample on the necks of kings, and hang up their dead bodies on gibbets . . . It would therefore have been contrary to the feelings of humanity to exult in their ignominy, had God not so ordered it. But as such was his pleasure, it behoves us to acquiesce in his decision, without presuming to inquire why he was so severe.[13]

But it is all too common to assume that, on the one hand, Calvin represents the only kind of Christian voice on the matter in which the value and perhaps truth of the Bible is upheld, and, on the other hand, that Bainton, for example, is correct in his analysis of the role of texts such as Joshua in a bloody history of the church. Both these points seem so plausible – that, roughly speaking, Calvin represents the only kind of 'sound' Christian voice, and that the book of Joshua has often provided the warrant for religiously motivated violence, and the Crusades in particular.

But both these very plausible assumptions are in fact incorrect – traditionally Joshua was not usually read in the way that Calvin read it, and traditionally Joshua has seldom been used to justify violence in the name of God. Very little of the material relating to the justification or preaching of the Crusades, for example, made any reference to Joshua. As a matter of fact, the gospels played a far more prominent role in justifying the Crusades than the book of Joshua, which is conspicuous by its absence.[14] It seems that Bainton, and those that have used his work, simply assumed this since it seems so plausible.

## Remembering the forgotten pathways: Listening to Origen

So what other ways might there be of reading Joshua in a faith-ful way as a Christian? To consider this question we must go back further in the history of the Church to the third century, and look to Origen, whose reading of Joshua became, gener-ally speaking, the standard way of interpreting it as Christian Scripture at least until the time of the Reformation. How then did Origen, and the 'premodern' church, tend to read Scripture? Did they trust it as the word of God? Were they unaware and naïve in relation to historical and ethical difficul-ties? Well, Scripture was certainly trusted as the word of God. And whilst the premoderns were unaware of many of the his-torical and archaeological issues that we are now aware of, it is clear that they were well aware of historical and ethical diffi-culties in Old Testament narratives. But precisely because they had an unswerving trust in Scripture, an awareness of histori-cal and ethical difficulties in the narratives did not lead to a crisis of faith or to a rejection of problematic texts. Rather, the premoderns were led to understand texts with difficulties like these as having their real meaning somewhere other than in the 'literal' or 'plain' sense of the text (i.e., what the text seems to say 'at face value'), the level where the ethical and historical difficulties are located. The ethical and historical difficulties in a text were, therefore, cues to the reader of the text to seek the significance of the text in a 'spiritual sense'.[15] Origen, for exam-ple, was well aware that there were 'historical difficulties' in Scripture, but used them as a 'hermeneutical cue' to seek the value and truth of Scripture in something other than its 'his-toricity'.

Let us look at an example in Joshua. The narrator's note that Rahab's house is in the wall of Jericho (Josh. 2:15) sits rather uneasily with the famous collapse of Jericho's wall and saving of Rahab in Joshua 6 when coupled with the comment that she and her family were to remain in her house when Jericho was attacked (Josh. 2:18–19). One might of course seek to 'harmo-nize' the texts by appealing to the miraculous preservation of her house, or to the wall only partly collapsing, or perhaps, as the rabbis did, by appealing to ingenious schemes of city wall construction that would allow for her house to remain intact when the wall fell. But none of these ingenious solutions actually reflect *what the text tells us*. They are attempts to force the significance of the narrative and its understanding into historical terms. In some ways, such harmonizing strategies can actually 'damage' the narrative. For it seems that the point of the wall collapse is to testify to the power of God to bring Jericho's wall down *completely*, removing it completely as an obstacle, thus 'talking up' the miraculous dimension of the story. Indeed, I rather like traditional Jewish renderings of the account in which the walls do not 'tumble down' but sink into the ground, indicating their *complete* removal – something that is a possible rendering of the Hebrew of Joshua 6. In other words, to appeal to a partial wall collapse to 'save the historicity' of the account seems to move away from a significant point of the story. Therefore it seems quite possible that the location of Rahab's house might well be precisely the sort of 'stumbling block' that Origen talks about that urges us to move away from seeing the value and purpose of these stories in terms of their 'historicity'. Another example can be seen when one considers the nature of the so-called 'spy mission' of Joshua 2 – the spies only go to a prostitute's house and return to Joshua without any 'intelligence'. So it seems that it is all the more likely that these narratives are seeking to do something other than be historical reports. For why have a spy mission that does not result in the gain of any intelligence?

Regarding the ethical difficulties, in his homily on the ethically difficult Joshua 10:20–26 Origen remarks,

> But Marcion and Valentinus and Basilides and the other heretics with them, since they refuse to understand these things in a manner worthy of the Holy Spirit, 'deviated from the faith and became devoted to many impieties,' [1 Tim. 6:10] bringing forth another God of the Law, both creator and judge of the world, who teaches a certain cruelty through these things that are written. For example, they are ordered to trample upon the necks of their enemies and to suspend from wood the kings of that land that they violently invade.

And yet, if only my Lord Jesus the Son of God would grant that to me and order me to crush the spirit of fornication with my feet and trample upon the necks of the spirit of wrath and rage, to trample on the demon of avarice, to trample down boasting, to crush the spirit of arrogance with my feet, and, when I have done all these things, not to hang the most exalted of these exploits upon myself but upon his cross. Thereby I imitate Paul, who says, 'the world is crucified to me,' [Gal. 6:14] and, that which we have already related above, 'Not I, but the grace of God that is in me' [1 Cor. 15:10].

But if I deserve to act thus, I shall be blessed and what Jesus [Joshua] said to the ancients will also be said to me, 'Go courageously and be strengthened; do not be afraid nor be awed by their appearance, because the Lord God has delivered all your enemies into your hands' [Josh. 10:25] If we understand these things spiritually and manage wars of this type spiritually and if we drive out all those spiritual iniquities from heaven, then we shall be able at last to receive from Jesus as a share of the inheritance even those places and kingdoms that are the kingdoms of heaven, bestowed by our Lord and Savior Jesus Christ, 'to whom is the glory and the dominion forever and ever. Amen!' [1 Pet. 4:11][16]

What is interesting here is that Origen's non-literal approach to the text operated precisely *in contrast* to the interpretative practices of the Gnostic 'heretics' (Marcion, Valentinus and Basilides) who asserted that the Old Testament must be understood 'literally'. Origen's reading here is strikingly different from Calvin's (compare Calvin's reading of 10:18 above), and ironically Calvin's reading of this text appears to be closer to the Gnostic heretics than to Origen's! Moreover, Origen's approach seems to start precisely with the same kind of probing of the text as the postcolonialist might – there is a recognition and acceptance of the fact that the text seems ethically problematic as it stands! So again, for Origen difficulties in the text – this time of an ethical nature – are cues to seek the significance of the text somewhere other than in its sense as a literal description of events. Perhaps then contemporary postcolonial and ethical-critical, as well as historical-critical readings of

Scripture may actually function as calls back to a more faithful reading of Scripture.

This approach was by no means limited to Origen or to the book of Joshua. In another ethically difficult passage, the plundering of the Egyptians in the book of Exodus, Gregory of Nyssa, in the fourth century work *The Life of Moses* suggests,

> Do not be surprised at all if both things – the death of the first-born and the pouring out of the blood – did not happen to the Israelites and on that account reject the contemplation which we have proposed concerning the destruction of evil as if it were a fabrication without any truth.[17]

Indeed, it is clear that this kind of approach – a 'spiritual' or perhaps 'allegorical' approach to the text coupled with a recognition of the difficulties of texts such as Joshua at the 'literal level' – was widespread in the premodern period. For example, in the mediaeval *glossa ordinaria*, a compendium of established readings and notes on the biblical text, readings such as Origen's and others similar to Origen's dominate. It was quite possibly the pervasive influence of the traditional reading of Joshua that stopped Christians from using Joshua to justify violence.[18] In other words, rather than Calvin's reading being standard for faithful Christian reading of Joshua, it marks only one of several approaches to reading Old Testament texts in the Christian tradition in its insistence on the 'literal sense'. In fact Calvin's reading seems to represent something of a break with established reading practices of Scripture, a break that was to become standard in modernity, which led in the end to historical and ethical criticism of Scripture and thus to the problems with which we started this chapter.

It is worth noting that in Origen's homily on Joshua 10:20–26 (cited above) what is implied in his critique of the 'heretics' is that they misinterpreted the text because they read it in a manner unworthy of the Holy Spirit, a manner that 'deviated from the faith'. This is rather like the kind of approach that Irenaeus took against the same heretics in the second century in *Against the Heretics* in order to argue that they were misreading Scripture. For Irenaeus the argument is that scriptural texts are read as parts of a whole, as parts of the body of Scripture[19] understood through the tradition that was passed down from the apostles.[20] So, Irenaeus, and later Origen, were confident of a generally correct reading of Scripture because they were reading the texts in their correct context traditionally and thus theologically (i.e., 'in a manner worthy of the Holy Spirit'). But this 'correct context' was *not* the original context of the text or what it 'originally meant'. Rather, it was the context of a text within Scripture as a whole *and* within the apostolic tradition in which these texts were received and used. So, for example, Scripture speaks of a loving God and of love for neighbour – whoever that might be according to the parable of the Good Samaritan. So the question is then raised as to whether Joshua is read well in terms of a God who commands genocide, if Joshua is read as being connected with the whole of Scripture and the teaching of Jesus, with the answer to the question seeming to be 'no'. In other words, reading Joshua 10:20–26 in the way that Origen does (cited above) is a way of reading the text that (a) 'fits' with the Bible as a whole as per Origen's concern and (b) the received Christian theological tradition passed down from the apostles, as per Irenaeus who was particularly concerned with rooting this 'rule of faith' in the public teaching of the apostles.

The approach of Irenaeus, that scriptural texts are understood in the light of a tradition, actually sounds quite 'postmodern' – the context of the interpreter within a tradition is recognized to be important. This practise of reading-within-the-tradition was something that was valued in the early church, as we see in the debate between Irenaeus and the Gnostics. Both Irenaeus and the Gnostics read the scriptural texts within the context of different traditions, resulting in differing understandings of the texts. So it is likely that if one seeks to read Joshua in isolation from the remainder of Scripture, or in isolation from the context of its use within the church, then it will be misread.[21] The context of the interpreter, and the 'interpretative community' of which they are a part is important. So perhaps one might say that where Marcion's approach, and many modern and postmodern approaches to the text go wrong is that they read the text 'in the wrong context', even though they ask the important questions of the text, such as questions regarding its morality. They ask the right questions, but point in the wrong direction for an answer. Indeed, it is interesting that Marcion's famous problem with the Old Testament – that it portrays a vengeful God different from the God of the New Testament – sounds very similar to contemporary interpretations of texts like Joshua. For Marcion, and for many contemporary readers such as Mbuwayesango, the answer to the difficulties raised by texts like Joshua is the rejection of the texts. For other Christians the answer is found in Calvin's reading – we must simply give up our ideas about morality in relation to God, as we are sinful humans before a transcendent God.[22] But for figures such as Irenaeus, Origen and Gregory of Nyssa there is a different answer. They point us to a different way of reading texts such as Joshua. Are they right? Is their approach convincing?

Allegorical and spiritual reading, as found in figures such as Origen and Gregory of Nyssa often receives 'bad press' for being wild and lacking control. However, it is easy to exaggerate how unruly spiritual reading was. If one looks at the way that, for example, Rahab's story has been traditionally interpreted and used, readings of the story tend to cluster around a common core. One does not find anything wildly different from Hebrews 11:31 or James 2:25 for example, where she is seen as exemplifying or embodying faith. Nevertheless, it is fair to say that much allegorical reading often seems rather 'atomistic' (in that it develops a small detail in a story and not the story as a whole) and is unconvincing in its details.[23] It is not unproblematic, and one cannot simply 'return' to a pre-modern interpretation of Joshua and reassert it today. In other words, whilst Rahab's story might be read well in terms of what 'faith' ought to look like, it is possibly not a good reading of the text to see in the scarlet cord that she hangs from her window (Josh. 2:18) a foreshadowing of the blood of Christ.

So we need to consider what it might mean to read Old Testament texts well, especially in new contexts (i.e., reading the ancient Israelite text of Joshua in a Christian context). Should we read Joshua in terms of history and ethics at the 'literal level' of the text, or do problems in these areas suggest that it ought to be read in a different way altogether; a way that might make statements such as Joshua 10:40 ('So Joshua defeated the whole land . . . he left no one remaining, but utterly destroyed all that breathed, as the LORD God of Israel commanded.') look rather different? My goal in this book is to argue that the traditional Christian ways of reading Scripture can be reworked for our own context.

# 2.

# On Wearing Good Glasses:
# The Importance of Interpretation

In chapter 1 we saw that concerns with historical and ethical difficulties might point us to a new (or renewed) way of reading Old Testament texts. The Church Fathers suggest to us that historical and ethical difficulties in a narrative might be indicators to us that we misread an Old Testament text if we read it primarily in terms of historical or ethical description via the 'plain sense' of the text. The Fathers mapped out a whole other way of reading the texts in a theologically faithful scheme, but a scheme that is perhaps unconvincing in a number of its details today. One could, therefore, reject the scheme, or one could ask if whether in fact the instincts of the Church Fathers were basically correct in moving towards reading some texts 'non-literally', but in a non-literal sense that needs to be constructed and understood in another way today.

Returning to the issue of 'literary approaches' to the Bible that was introduced in chapter 1, I think that it is uncontroversial to say that literary readings of Old Testament narratives have been very fruitful. Literary approaches take as their starting point that the Bible is 'literature', and that by studying the way in which literature is composed and functions more generally one may better understand what is going on in the narratives of the Bible. This approach has, however, attracted some critics who are concerned that the Bible is surely 'more than' any other literature. That the Bible is 'more than' other literature – even great literature such as Shakespeare – is uncontroversial for the Christian. But whilst the Bible is 'more than' other literature, it is still, nonetheless, great literature, and not 'less than' other great literature. As the Bible shares the features of 'great literature' with other material (however unique it also is), it would seem likely that studying the way in which literature is composed, conveys meaning and functions in general terms is likely to help us to understand the literature of the Bible better. Theologically speaking, Scripture has a human dimension which is not 'totally other' than the human dimensions of other literature. At a bare minimum, language, grammar and syntax are shared by biblical texts and other texts. Other features that are shared are those such as plot and characterization. And the results of literary readings of the Bible over the past twenty years or so speak for themselves – we have a far greater appreciation of the nature and meaning of the biblical texts in the light of literary approaches to them.

## Turning to Anthropology for help

I would like to take this process of reflection on general human modes of communication, learning and development a stage further. I wish to move our focus into the realm of anthropology, and in particular, anthropological approaches to the kind of literature that shapes the identities of communities – communities that might be small tribes or large nations. Important literature does not simply tell an entertaining story – it shapes the lives of individuals and communities. In the same way that the biblical text has a 'human' dimension that it shares with other literature, the function of the biblical text has a 'human dimension' in shaping the life of a community – originally an ancient Israelite community in the case of Joshua, but now also Jews and Christians who cherish this text. In other words, Joshua, along with the Bible, is a narrative (or set of narratives and related texts) that 'seeks' to shape the existence and life of a community in response to the manifestation and discernment of a gracious God.[1] The biblical narratives are constructed so as to function in drawing people and communities into closer relationship with God and ever more faithful response to him. Indeed, for the Christian reader of Scripture the function of Scripture must finally be to draw the reader into closer communion with God as this is worked out in daily life. So Scripture, as a collection of narratives, certainly does not do 'less than' shaping the life of people and communities, even if Scripture might be said to do 'more than' shaping the life of the community as any important narrative might for any community. As I have just suggested, it is widely accepted that Scripture is not 'less than' literature and that it is fruitful to consider the ways in which literature works in general so as to better understand how to read the Bible more sensitively. In the same way it is likely that a study of the ways in which narratives shape the lives of communities in general will help us to better understand how the Bible 'seeks' to shape the life of the Christian community, and thus show us how to interpret and use it more appropriately.

### 'Myth' – an aid or a stumbling block?

So, how do narratives shape the lives of communities in general terms, and what tools are available to study this? This is where we need to turn to contemporary anthropology. But here we hit a problem – or rather a *perceived* problem. And that problem is that the term that contemporary anthropologists have tended to use to describe narratives that shape the lives of communities is the term 'myth'. And here the alarm bells ring for many! How can the Bible be thought of as being comparable with 'myth'? Many Christians will want to run a mile here, especially in the light of texts such as 1 Timothy 1:4; 2 Timothy 4:4 and 2 Peter 1:16. Surely myths are old wives tales, primitive science, naïve stories, or expressions of a false consciousness? Or, to put it another way, aren't myths simply deluded untruths? This is certainly the way that the term 'myth' was used in the nineteenth century, and in the vernacular in the twentieth century. Understandably the use of the term 'myth' has often been avoided in relation to the Bible. But the issue is that the usage of the term 'myth' has 'slipped' – contemporary anthropologists mean something different by it from what it has popularly come to mean, and something different from the way that it is used in the Bible. I wish that a new term had been adopted, but it has not. During the twentieth century anthropologists began to do more subtle and careful work on the ways in which narratives shape the lives of communities whilst keeping the term 'myth' to describe such narratives. So in much anthropological analysis the term 'myth' lost its bad overtones to become simply a term used to describe the way in which the identity and existence of individuals and communities is shaped and constructed, whether well or badly, truthfully or untruthfully, scientifically or unscientifically. Thus on balance it seems best to stick with the term 'myth', but be fully aware that we are using it in a different sense from how it is popularly understood.

But a further difficulty is that anthropologists working in different fields and disciplines tended to consider the way that narratives shape identity with regard to their own discipline only. So those concerned with psychology studied narratives in psychological perspective only; those concerned with politics and ideology considered the narratives in these terms only; those concerned with ritual considered the narratives in terms of ritual only, and so on. So by the end of the twentieth century, in professional and academic circles there existed a multitude of different approaches to myth – a plethora of competing attempts to describe how narratives in fact shape and construct the life of a community.

Myth is a problematic term with both a problematic 'history of use' and contemporary use, in that it is rather poorly defined. But it is a mistake to think that we are now 'isolated' from myth, or that we have 'come of age' and moved beyond it for we are all shaped by what might be termed 'myth' even though we might not recognize or label it as such. Robert Segal, in a recent, very readable introduction to myth, notes that for the anthropologist Mircea Eliade myth is all around us, and all around all cultures today – it is simply camouflaged. Segal goes on to show how, for example, stories relating to John F. Kennedy Jr. and George Washington might be said to reflect contemporary myth that constructs identity in American society.[2]

## Understanding 'myth'

So what is 'myth' then? Given the difficulties that I have outlined, venturing a definition is problematic. Perhaps a better
way of approaching the question is not that of, 'What is myth?'
but the question, 'How do we shape our lives and respond to
the world around us?' Still, towards the end of the twentieth
century there has been a tendency to try to draw together different approaches to myth to provide a rich and full account of
how we do indeed 'shape our lives' and try to make sense of
the world. One such approach is that of William Doty, who
seeks to define myth via the following rather complicated
statement:

> A mythological corpus consists of (1) a usually complex net-
> work of myths that are (2) culturally important (3) imaginal (4)
> stories, conveying by means of (5) metaphoric and symbolic
> diction, (6) graphic imagery, and (7) emotional conviction and
> participation, (8) the primal, foundational accounts (9) of
> aspects of the real, experienced world and (10) humankind's
> roles and relative statuses within it.
>
> Mythologies may (11) convey the political and moral values
> of a culture and (12) provide systems of interpreting (13) indi-
> vidual experience within a universal perspective, which may
> include (14) the intervention of suprahuman entities as well as
> (15) aspects of the natural and cultural orders. Myths may be
> enacted or reflected in (16) rituals, ceremonies, and dramas,
> and (17) they may provide materials for secondary elaboration,
> the constituent mythemes (mythic units) having become mere-
> ly images or reference points for a subsequent story, such as a
> folktale, historical legend, novella, or prophecy.[3]

In other words, for Doty myths form a network of important
symbolic stories that address the heart as well as the head so
as to evoke ways of making sense of and living in a particular
community. Sometimes myths have political dimensions,
involve gods, relate to rituals and/or provide the basis for further important stories. At one level this is an attractive
approach, drawing together different areas of the study of

myth into a unified whole. But at another level it is problematic as it represents something of a combination of different
understandings of myth that reflect different understandings
of how people shape and construct their lives. So it is not clear
that Doty's definition does not combine possibly contradictory
approaches. However, it is worth saying that in theological
perspective it is quite likely that a 'thick description' of how
people construct their identity will be required. The Christian
tradition has continually suggested that human identity is constructed in rational/intellectual ('head level') and emotional/
affective ('heart level') terms, for example, and so any
approach that does not account for both is likely to be rather
'thin' and partial. Likewise humans are social and relational in
nature, and so any account of how identity is shaped is likely
to require sociological and ideological dimensions too. So
despite its difficulties, Doty's definition seems useful here as a
*starting* point (even though I do not wish to adopt it as a formal definition) since it gives an idea of the *sort* of thing that we
are talking about when we are discussing myth. But it is worth
pointing out that Doty's definition says nothing about how a
myth might relate to history – and this is a feature of much
contemporary work on myth. Myth is no longer set in opposition to history – rather, myth is seen as being ambivalent
towards actual historical events. A myth may or not narrate
events that 'actually happened'. It is also worth saying here
that *myths are narratives that are often set in 'prototypical' times –*
i.e., in times that are *foundational to the life of a community.*
Setting a narrative in such a time (whether it is an accurate
'historical' description or not) confers authority and importance on the kind of identity that the narrative seeks to construct, for it implies that such identity is foundational to and
inherent in the community's existence. And of course Joshua is
set in a foundational time for Israel's existence – her entrance
to the land. We can thus expect Joshua to seek to communicate
what is inherent in Israel's identity.

Indeed, before we go any further let us consider how all this
might actually help in the task of understanding Scripture better. To use a 'happier' vocabulary, studying from this perspective of myth helps us with regard to the question of genre of

texts. What kind of material do we have in front of us in a text like Joshua, and how does it function to shape us in response to God? In chapter 1 we saw that historical and ethical difficulties were cues to seek the significance of a text like Joshua somewhere other than in its 'plain' or 'literal' sense as description of the world. The sort of anthropological approach that I am proposing here suggests that it is quite likely that the genre of a text like Joshua is, as discovered through comparison with other texts that are designed to shape identity, one that is concerned with symbolism, with existential questions of life and with conveying values through story. This will all need to be teased out, although it is a pointer as to where we are heading. Might one initially say then that *the historical and ethical difficulties point us not necessarily to an allegorical or spiritual sense of a text, but rather to a symbolic sense that has theological and spiritual implications?*

How might we develop these ideas? A few general comments are in order in relation to various recent approaches to myth. Both political/ideological and psychological approaches to myth have grown strongly in the twentieth century, with very different approaches having been developed by different psychologists for example. But the growth of such approaches indicates the importance of ideology and psychology in relation to the shaping of human identity. Theologically speaking this should not be surprising. We have a clear psychological dimension to us with aspects of our character and our inner drives that are somewhat hidden and obscure to us (e.g. Jer. 17:9). Moreover, it is clear that humans are created to live in community and that there are theologically faithful and unfaithful ways in which we can relate to each other, and to various groups, within community. Therefore we ought to expect narratives that shape the identity of the Christian and the Christian community to reflect ideological and psychological concerns – and these concerns are properly aspects of the 'theology' of the narrative.

The ideological dimensions will be developed later as they are complex, but for now I simply wish to draw attention to one aspect of Joshua in psychological perspective, and that is the issue of desire, and how it is in a sense 'beneath the surface' of Joshua. What is it that Joshua reflects the desire for? Is it a desire for genocide and destruction? Surprisingly, for Joshua what is desired is 'rest' (Heb. *nuach*, Josh. 1:13, 15; 21:44; 22:4 and 23:1). In these important summary statements it is 'rest' that God promises, and, in psychological perspective, rest is what Israel desires. The promise and desire is thus for peace and not war, and so Joshua might then be seen as fundamentally about achieving peace and rest rather than being about warfare. In a sense then, this is a concept – that of finding rest – that is ripe for eschatological development, which is indeed what happens with the idea of *nuach* ('rest') in the prophetic literature (Isa. 14:3, 7; 11:20; 28:12; 32:18, and cf. Dan. 12:13).[4]

### 'Myth' and symbol

Having thought about some general aspects of myth, let us turn to the specific idea of symbol. Myth and symbol are interrelated concepts, and the idea of 'symbol' is as difficult to pin down as that of myth – myths and symbols often interpret each other. Myths are often built around symbols and convey meaning through symbols and help interpret what is important about particular symbols. But the idea of what constitutes a symbol is contested. Some would see 'symbol' as being synonymous with 'sign' – an arbitrary pointer to something else, such as certain road signs. But I think that it is preferable to seek a 'richer' account of symbol. So for example a lion might symbolize strength. But a lion might also symbolize grandeur, or, drawing these ideas together, a lion might symbolize kingship perhaps. In other words, something that is tangible or 'concrete' and familiar is used to evoke ideas that are (often) more abstract, or at least more difficult to 'get hold of'. There is a sense in which what is tangible 'shares in' or points towards – or symbolizes – what is less tangible. The familiar evokes ideas of what is less familiar, in an attempt to clarify or say something new about the less familiar, often in a way that engages the emotions as well as the intellect. An image of a lion 'says' something about kingship that a dictionary definition of the role of a king does not. But as in the case of the image of a lion, a symbol can symbolize different things depending on the context that it is used in.

So with symbols we can speak of there being two senses to a symbol – the 'literal' or 'manifest' or 'concrete' or 'first-order' sense, and a 'non-literal' or 'opaque' or 'figurative' or 'second-order' sense that the first-order sense gestures towards. So, when a lion is used as a symbol, its first-order sense is that the symbol means a lion, an image which evokes a number of second-order senses such as strength, grandeur or kingship. The concrete image of the lion evokes and says something new, in a way that is difficult to define in a propositional sense, about strength, grandeur and kingship. Symbols thus have an 'existential' significance, working at intellectual (head) and affectual (heart) levels, and give rise to a plenitude of new ways of imaginative perception, which is perhaps why they are so prevalent in prophetic and poetic literature in the Bible – such as in Ezekiel's vision of the valley of the dry bones (Ezek. 37), where the symbolism of the restoration of the skeletons to life can be used powerfully to evoke the restoration of Israel or the resurrection of the body in a way that goes beyond simple description of these phenomena. So as well as being able to teach us about concepts that are difficult to grasp, symbols also teach in a way that engages the imagination and emotions, making them more potent than a certain kind of description by propositions.[5]

But how does all this rather abstract discussion help us with Joshua? Let us take the example of Rahab, and her story in Joshua 2. Rahab is a Canaanite, and a prostitute. In a powerful way she can be said to symbolize the 'outsider' to Israel (cf. Deut. 7:1–5) in that her characteristics share or even partake in the characteristics of the outsider. But more than this, note that Josh 2:1 commences with the note that Joshua sends spies from Shittim, who proceed straight to Rahab's house. This note evokes Numbers 25, where Israel is reported as staying in Shittim, and beginning to indulge in sexual immorality with Moabite women, leading to the worship of other gods (Num. 25:1–3) – precisely the concern of Deuteronomy 7:1–5. So in other words Rahab, in the context of the story in Joshua 2 and in the context of the Pentateuch, evokes all the fears and worries associated with outsiders and the effect that they will have on Israel. The story encourages the reader to tremble as well as to think, encouraging more wholehearted engagement on the part of the reader. Rahab symbolizes the outsider in an existentially powerful way. So in context the character of Rahab is a powerful symbol. But in another context she might symbolize something very different. Indeed, postcolonial approaches to Joshua highlight the observation that if Joshua is read through 'Canaanite eyes' then Rahab symbolizes the traitor who betrays her people. In other words she symbolizes or existentially evokes something quite different in a Canaanite context from an Israelite context. Thus we see how symbols evoke an existential participation in 'something more', but it is a contextual rather than a universal evocation. What a symbol means will vary from context to context, but its meaning is stable, even if not unique, and more than simply conventional, in any given context. We may recall Irenaeus' comments in chapter 1 and our discussion there, in that to read a narrative well it needs to be read in the right context in order to be read responsibly and well. To read Joshua with 'Canaanite eyes' is to read it in the wrong context for shaping Israelite or Christian identity, for it is designed to shape the identity of a community from within the context of that community. The significance of the symbolism will be missed as we can see. To put it rather crudely another way, if one uses something for the wrong purpose, one should not be surprised if it does not work.

To take another example, Daniel Hawk's comments on the Jordan crossing in Joshua 3–4 demonstrate again how attention to symbol is illuminative for reading Joshua. He suggests that the story of the crossing has a 'mythic quality' and is symbolic of Israel's transformation from a disordered people in the wilderness to an ordered people in the Promised Land, with the land symbolizing a 'total social order':

> By crossing the Jordan, Israel enters a bounded place and leaves the vast expanse of the wilderness. The transformation is made possible by Yahweh, 'frame-maker, boundary-keeper and master of transformations' . . . who, represented by the Ark, stands between chaos and ordered existence. The narrative thus

accentuates the liturgical elements of the episode in order to focus the reader's attention on the symbolic significance of the boundary being traversed. The priests, who oversee Israel's maintenance and traversing of boundaries, stand, appropriately, in the middle of the border-region to mediate journey of the entire people from wilderness to promised land. Extensive preparations are undertaken to ensure that the crossing is made in an orderly and integrated manner (3:1–13), and this is precisely what is done. Throughout the episode, the ostensive plot depicts the Jordan crossing in terms of wholes and boundaries. Thus Israel as a people has crossed over into a new, ordered existence with Yahweh (who confirms the transformation with a miraculous stoppage of the water).[6]

We shall develop this later. But for now let us simply note that even the promised land itself takes on a symbolic quality, evoking life with Yahweh in the covenant and the blessings associated with this life. Life in the land is a sharing or participation in this life with Yahweh, even if it is not the same as life with Yahweh. If one combines this observation with our remarks above on the importance of 'rest' in Joshua, where rest evokes an eschatological desire and goal, then some traditional readings of Joshua become intelligible:

> But in Scripture sometimes God, in conferring all these earthly benefits on them [the Israelites], determined to lead them by his own hand to the hope of heavenly things . . . [I]n the earthly possession [the Israelites] enjoyed, they looked, as in a mirror, upon the future inheritance they believed to have been prepared for them in heaven.[7]

In other words, for the Christian reader entrance into the land can evoke entrance into the new life that God gives in Christ as the symbolism is interpreted in a new context, new life that awaits a final eschatological consummation.

These sorts of interpretation reflect what happens when symbols are working well. Symbols evoke existential meanings developed in myths that go beyond the sense of the symbol as literal description itself as the context of the symbol's use expands. In other words the land here as a symbol reflects more than land, evoking more than geography. Symbols do not have a single meaning, but give rise to a number of meanings, albeit meanings that cluster around a common core – they have a 'surplus of meaning'. So, for example, the Christian use of the symbol of the land develops naturally out of its earlier use in an Israelite context. (We will return to the question of what counts as 'good use' of symbols later.)

However, symbols, metaphors and myths, whilst initially having such creative and evocative power, can, and often do, become 'tired' or 'dead', or, as Doty puts it, they 'become locked into single-meaning codes, where each term "stands for" only one meaning'.[8] And this is crucially important for Joshua, being precisely what has happened with the text, and why it has become so problematic. Its second-order symbolic sense – the sense where its existential edge and importance lies – has been lost in favour of a collapsing of its meaning into its literal or first-order sense. (This can be illustrated with the example of the lion. When the symbolic significance of the picture of a lion is lost, a lion no longer conjures up images of grandeur or kingship, but simply a large four-legged animal.) Joshua has come to be seen as a historical account of Israel's conquest of Canaan, and its significance has been explored in these terms, with its genre not being respected, with all the problems that go with this coming to the fore in the twentieth century in terms of archaeology and ethics. We will have to wait to discover just what one might mean by Joshua's overall symbolic sense, but for now we see at least how an appreciation of symbol can help us to understand Joshua's 'loss of meaning'. I think it is quite proper to call the evocation of meaning of symbols in Scripture 'revelatory', and thus by losing this symbolic dimension of evocation through attempting to understand the narrative as a straightforward report of history violence has been done to the revelatory character of Joshua. Joshua ceases to be a 'revelatory text' if we never move beyond its 'face value' meaning. As I suggested earlier, one might say that the symbolic sense of reading developed here can be said to be rather like the 'spiritual' sense of the early church, with the evocation and development of the symbolic sense being a genuinely 'spiritual' or 'Spirit-filled' activity.

In a sense then, what a scriptural 'mythical narrative' presents us with is a symbolic, revelatory 'world of the text' that invites us as individuals and communities to be imaginatively transformed and shaped by such a world into more faithful and fuller relationship with God worked out in everyday life. Such a narrative is not *primarily* a 'historical *description*' of the world, but rather a 'prophetic *redescription*' of the world that we are encouraged to participate in. The question to ask is not then that of whether a text such as Joshua provides an accurate historical description of past events, but rather of whether it provides a faithful and fitting invitation to a world that encourages fuller and more transparent participation with life in God.

### Victor Turner and myth

But how then, one naturally asks, can a text that has as its world a world of genocide and destruction in any way invite one to a fuller relationship with a loving and compassionate God? This is where the work of the anthropologist Victor Turner is important, for his work gives pointers as to how the 'world of the text' might or might not be existentially appropriated and enacted – that is, how one might imaginatively use the text to shape one's attitudes, feelings, conscience and the way that one lives and acts in daily life. For Turner myths are associated with performance, often being associated with ritual. But he has developed and extended the concepts of 'ritual' and 'performance' to encompass the 'enaction' of *social actions* in daily life.[9] Our lives are 'performances' in effect, 'performances' that are shaped by the myths that pervade our societies. Importantly, Turner remarks that myths

> involve a restructuring of social relationships – with the possibility of conflict and disorder. The well-known amorality of myths is intimately connected with their existential bearing. The myth does not describe what ought to be done . . . Liminal symbolism [that is, symbolism associated with ambiguous

phases of transition or the bridging of differing categories such as human/divine], both in its ritual and mythic expressions, abounds in direct or figurative transgressions of the moral codes that hold good in secular life, such as human sacrifice, human flesh eating, and incestuous unions of brother-sister or mother-son deities or their human representatives. Thus the theory that myths are paradigmatic (Eliade 1957) or that myths afford precedents and sanctions for social status and moral rules (Malinowski 1925) requires some sort of qualification. Myths and liminal rites are not to be treated as models for secular behavior. Nor, on the other hand, are they to be regarded as cautionary tales, as negative models which should not be followed . . . Liminality is pure potency, where anything can happen, where immoderacy is normal, even normative, and where the elements of culture and society are released from their customary configurations and recombined in bizarre and terrifying imagery. Yet this boundlessness is restricted – although never without a sense of hazard – by the knowledge that this is a unique situation and by a definition of the situation which states that the rites and myths must be told in a prescribed order and in a symbolic rather than a literal form. The very symbol that expresses at the same time restrains; through mimesis there is an acting out – rather than the acting – of an impulse that is biologically motivated but socially and morally reprehended.[10]

So myths for Turner have symbolic and existential characteristics and are to be 'enacted', but not in any *straightforward* way as 'models to follow'. To take a somewhat trivial (but accessible) example, perhaps one could say that contemporary novels provide mythical portrayals of certain aspects of life (such as ambiguous phases of transitions in relationships) that affect the way in which many people 'enact' their lives. But many people would not necessarily regard the behaviour and actions narrated in such novels as 'models' to follow as such, even if novels do sometimes provide examples of role-models. This idea of enaction provides an important perspective on the idea of the 'world of the text', and on the way that mythical texts might invite us to shape 'our world' and the way that we live and act.

How does this work out with Joshua? There are a number of commands to 'utterly destroy' the inhabitants of the land, and a number of reports of the fulfilment of this command, a command that reflects Deuteronomy 7:1–5. The Hebrew word underlying this is a specific term, *herem*. *Herem* has often been interpreted using the idea of 'holy war'. We shall consider the question of what *herem* means in the next chapter, but for now, it is worth noting that Turner's comments might suggest that *its significance should not be understood in terms of a description of the ethics and practice of ancient warfare, or as a 'model' to follow and 'act out' in daily life.* So perhaps *herem* could be understood in symbolic terms (in a sense that is yet to be clarified), leading to an enactment of the text that will look quite different from what one might think is implied when then text is read at face value. Clearly this is of key importance for Joshua, for it suggests that Joshua's concern is not that of a presentation of a certain kind of (un)ethical action at face value, in the same kind of way that it is not concerned with a literal description of history. So, we are now in a position to develop the quote from Karl Barth introduced in chapter 1 into the following:

> The idea that the Bible declares the Word of God only when it speaks *ethically or historically* is one which must be abandoned, especially in the Christian Church. One consequence of this misunderstanding was the great uncertainty of faith which resulted from an inability wholly to escape the impression that many elements in the Bible have the nature of *myth*, and an ignorance of where and how to draw the line which marks off what is finally *ethical or historical* and therefore the true Word of God. But in other cases it led to a rigid affirmation that in the Bible, as the Word of God, we have only "ethical" or "historical" accounts and no *myth* at all – an affirmation which can be sustained only if we either close our eyes or violently reinterpret what we see. In other cases again it resulted in an attempt to penetrate to an *"ethical" or "historical"* kernel which is supposed to give us the true, i.e., *"ethical" or "historical"* word of God – the only trouble being that in the process it was unfortunately found that with the discarding of myth we do lose not only a subsidiary theme but the main point at issue, i.e., the

biblical witness. We have to realise that in all three cases the presumed equation of the Word of God with an *"ethical"* or *"historical"* record is an inadmissible postulate which does not itself originate in the Bible at all but in the unfortunate habit of *contemporary* thought which assumes that the *validity and enduring significance of a narrative* stands or falls by whether it is *"ethical"* or *"historical"*.

How then might one think about how Joshua ought to be enacted? In particular, what might *herem* be symbolically expressive of, and how might *herem* be enacted? This is where it will be helpful to turn to other theories of myth so as to consider just what is going on in the symbolic world that Joshua constructs, perhaps in more intellectual and ideological dimensions. We have seen that Joshua is concerned with 'boundaries' in various ways – with what boundaries represent and what it menas to cross them. So we have considered the crossing of the Jordan as symbolizing crossing into a new way of life for Israel (Josh. 3–4). We have seen that Rahab symbolizes someone who is 'outside' the boundary of the community of Israel, but is someone who in some sense 'crosses' into the community of Israel (Josh. 2 and 6). Achan is someone who is 'inside' the boundary of Israel, yet symbolically crosses out of the community through death following disobedience (Josh. 7). So it would appear that much of the book of Joshua is concerned with questions of being inside or outside boundaries of various sorts, and how one moves across such boundaries, and what this means. How can we understand the role that these boundaries play and their nature? This is where we can turn to a recent approach to myth called *neo-structuralism* for help, because neo-structuralism provides a tool with which one can analyze just these sorts of concern.

## Neo-Structuralism and Myth

Neo-structuralism is Seth Kunin's development of the structuralist approach to myth of Claude Lévi-Strauss.[11] Structuralism is a cognitive and intellectual approach to the analysis of myth and society. It is based on the idea that people (often subconsciously) categorize or classify the world that they experience, and organize or relate the categories in such classification through various ideas of relation. Such classification or categorization often shows up, for instance, in terms of people groups – 'insiders' and 'outsiders', and the way in which they relate. So, for example, the inhabitants of a close-knit village community might (subconsciously) identify themselves as 'insiders' and all other people as 'outsiders', and develop ways of relating to outsiders: under what circumstances might an outsider become an insider – a true member of the community? By marriage? By living in the village for a certain number of years? By working there? Never? Structuralism in this case is concerned with the identification of this categorization of insider/outsider and the various relationships that exist between these categories. Or structuralism could be concerned with the classification of what is 'dirty' as opposed to what is 'clean', and how what is 'dirty' may become 'clean' for example, and how this plays out in society. Such classification may show up in some communities through the scrupulous avoidance of shoes that are worn outdoors (i.e. categorized as 'dirty, outside') being worn inside a house (i.e., 'clean, inside') for example, however 'dirty' the shoes might actually be.

However, the 'classical structuralism' of Lévi-Strauss has been criticized on a number of fronts. First, because it tends to dispense with 'meaning' in favour of 'underlying structure' – it is the existence of abstract categories and the way that they are related that is seen as significant in classical structuralism, rather than what the categories actually refer to in real life. So, in the example above, what is important in classical structuralism is the existence of the categories of 'inside' and 'outside' and the formal relations between them and not the nature of the categories in everyday life, i.e. what the village community is actually like or what might actually count as 'dirty'. Structuralist readings of biblical texts sometimes seem disappointing for this reason. For example, structuralism is often concerned with the *existence* of the categories of 'clean' and 'unclean' in Leviticus, and the relationships between them, rather than with the *content* of the categories – i.e., what they really mean for someone who wants to live life based on this book. Structuralism does not really address the question of which animals are unclean in particular, why they are unclean, or what difference this makes to everyday life for the Israelite. So, secondly, it has been criticized for its lack of attention to 'agency' in the construction of myths. So, for example, there may be little attention given to the *reason* for the classifications of 'clean' or 'unclean' in Leviticus, or what might be reflected in such categorization. In other words myths in structuralist perspective are seen as simply the expression of some sub-conscious phenomenon of classification, rather than the expression of some consciously created narrative to shape a community in a particular way. Finally, classical structuralism has been criticized for its 'cold intellectualism'.

Neo-structuralism is a development of structuralism that seeks to build on some of the fruitful results of structuralism, whilst modifying the approach to take account of its critics. Neo-structuralism retains the idea that societies the world over tend to 'structure' and categorize their understanding and view of the world, especially through their myths, around patterns of classification and relationships. The underlying 'structural categories' on which a given society is based in this sense are something that are 'recapitulated' throughout that society – the same patterns of categorization crop up again and again. This structure is given content at a narrative level in myths. So myths are expression of both a narrative and a structure, and can be analysed at narrative and structural levels, with both levels being important and inter-related. In neo-structuralist analysis the 'content' of the narrative retains a level of significance that tends to be lost in classical structuralist analysis. Finally, whilst structuralism focused attention on the subconscious aspects of myth, neo-structuralism, whilst not denying the importance of subconscious factors in the product of myth, is also concerned with *agency* in the production of myth – the conscious attempt to use myth to shape the ideology of a community.

Finally, it is worth noting that what neo-structuralist analysis identifies and builds upon are general tendencies and patterns of categorization. It does not offer precise rules that are valid in every case. In this sense it is rather like the wisdom that we find in Proverbs – general principles are offered rather than strict laws.

*Neo-structuralism applied to the Old and New Testaments*
Ancient Israelite structure is built upon a system of classification which has only two categories in which *mediation* and *transformation* between the categories is not permitted. So a person is either an Israelite or a non-Israelite; an Israelite is either a priest or a non-priest, and an animal is either clean or unclean. Transformation or mediation between these categories is impossible – an animal cannot be simultaneously clean and unclean (no mediation), and one is either born a priest or one is not (no transformation). In other words, the same basic categorization is replayed in different aspects of Israel's view of the world. But whereas structuralism was concerned with identifying the system of classification as abstractly as possible, neo-structuralism is concerned with the content and meaning of the classification and its development through conscious human agency expressed in narratives and their ongoing use in shaping the society. There is a two way 'conversation' between structural and narrative concerns, and neo-structuralism seeks to use this conversation in order to understand the narrative better through structure, and structure better through the narrative.

So, to take a concrete example in pictorial form at the 'structural level'

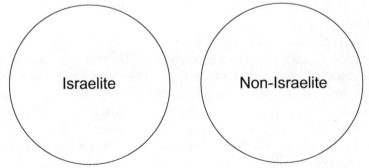

No mediation, no transformation
Every human being is categorized into one of the two circles.

**Figure 1: The 'structural level' – Ancient Israel**

And an example of this 'structure' being expressed at the 'narrative level' –

> After these things had been done, the officials approached me
> and said, 'The people of Israel, the priests, and the Levites have
> not separated themselves from the peoples of the lands with
> their abominations, from the Canaanites, the Hittites, the
> Perizzites, the Jebusites, the Ammonites, the Moabites, the
> Egyptians, and the Amorites. For they have taken some of their
> daughters as wives for themselves and for their sons. Thus the
> holy seed has mixed itself with the peoples of the lands, and in
> this faithlessness the officials and leaders have led the way.'
> When I heard this, I tore my garment and my mantle, and
> pulled hair from my head and beard, and sat appalled. (Ezra
> 9:1–3)

In other words, the 'myth' of the book of Ezra at the narrative
level reflects the structural level categorization of people into
'Israelite' and 'non-Israelite' with the implication that mediation and transformation are impossible. Marriage of a non-
Israelite to an Israelite here does not transform the
non-Israelite into an Israelite (or vice versa), and there is no
possibility expressed of any 'sharing' of the quality of
'Israelite' with that of 'non-Israelite' (no mediation, especially through offspring). So we can see how structure and
narrative relate, being expressed in what the neo-structuralist terms myth.

Neo-structuralism suggests that Israelite identity is ethnically or genealogically constructed (hence the importance of
genealogies in the Old Testament). This is the general tendency that neo-structuralism implies, as being something that
subconsciously pervades the society. But it is not a straightjacket – myths can be composed that represent a deliberate
attempt ideologically to challenge or 'push' such a structure in
new directions. Thus whilst one may infer that Israelite identity is, in general, genealogically constructed, stories of characters such as Ruth, Naaman (2 Kgs. 5), and, as we shall see,
Rahab, exist to 'push' the underlying ideology of the societal
structure to allow non-Israelites to be incorporated into Israel.

In the case of Ruth for example her story encourages the possibility of the transformation of the non-Israelite to the Israelite (Ruth 1:16).

What will turn out to be of crucial importance is that this 'pushing' of the underlying ideology of structure is central to the construction of Christian structure. In the Christian context, unlike the ancient Israelite context, mediation and transformation are possible – indeed, they are vital foundations for Christian identity. Christian identity, unlike ancient Israelite identity, is *based* upon transformation (conversion, from 'non-Christian' to 'Christian') and mediation (the indwelling of the divine Holy Spirit in human Christians who are yet sinners). We see examples in this radical shift in underlying structure expressed in, for example, the call to mission (i.e., non-Christians can convert to Christianity); in the abolishing of the distinction between clean and unclean animals; and in the Christian notion of the priesthood of all believers. So we see that ideas of transformation and mediation are recapitulated throughout Christian practice, and are one way of examining the discontinuity between the Old and New Testaments.

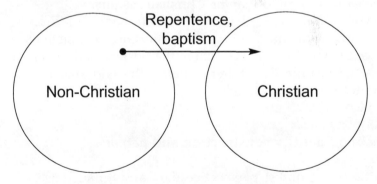

Categorizatioin with transformation

**Figure 2: The 'structural level' – Christian (I)**

Every human being is categorized into one of the two circles, but transformation is possible, expressed at the narrative level in texts such as Matthew 28:18–20 and Acts 2:38–39.

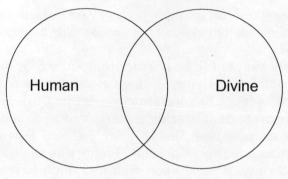

Categorization with mediation

**Figure 3: The 'structural level' – Christian (II)**

Christians, as humans, share in both human and divine qualities through the indwelling of the Holy Spirit. Mediation is
possible, expressed at the narrative level in texts such as
Romans 8:9–10. Thus transformation and mediation might be
said to express the nature of the Christian life – one seeks
transformation into increasing holiness and Christlikeness yet
one is always a sinner still. Transformation and mediation are,
therefore, central to shaping Christian identity.

We shall see later that it is precisely because Joshua is so
concerned with this pushing of identity construction in what is
essentially a 'Christian direction' that Joshua finds a very natural use within the church – hence the widespread use of
Joshua in the early church.

## Joshua, identity construction and *herem*

In neo-structuralist perspective then a myth such as Joshua
may be understood originally to be concerned with the jug-
gling of identity construction within the society of ancient
Israel – who are 'insiders' to the community ('true' Israelites)
and who are the 'outsiders'? What constitutes a true insider
(Israelite)? Can someone change status from insider to outsider, or vice versa? One then needs to consider what the significance of this is in the Christian context, in other words how

the myth of Joshua is *transformed* in significance in the Christian context. Indeed, as with symbolism, structuralist approaches to myth are often concerned with the transformations that occur when myths and symbols are used in new contexts and juxtaposed with other myths. Theologically speaking, and as the use of Joshua develops into the Christian context, these questions that Joshua raises can be re-considered in terms of what it is that constitutes faithful response to God in terms of an engaged relationship with him through Jesus, and how this is expressed in terms of relationships with others. But as the underlying structure of the Christian context is different from that of the ancient Israelite context as we have seen, some interesting shifts in the significance of the narrative are likely to occur, and we shall study these in chapter 5.

But for now let us note that in Joshua we are presented with a number of symbolically important characters whose stories reflect the sorts of question raised above. For example, we have Rahab, the ominous outsider who surprisingly 'confesses faith' like an Israelite insider and helps the Israelites; we have Achan, the ethnic Israelite insider who disobeys God, and acts like the outsider, and then we have the Gibeonites, who seem to have rather ambiguous qualities. It is the stories of these characters that make up much of the narrative of Joshua 1–12. What are these stories trying to do? How are they trying to shape response to God? These questions will dominate much of the following chapters, but in light of what we have said so far it seems that Joshua is trying to challenge and perhaps move away from the sort of shaping of identity implied in figure 1 above to that expressed in figures 2 and 3, which is one reason why Joshua is amenable to use in a Christian context, as I have suggested.

Furthermore, in the same way that Turner highlighted the amoral dimensions of myth in his work, Kunin observes how in many cases myths have amoral elements in the narrative because certain parts of such stories are required to serve structural level functions. Let me clarify this with an example. In the Patriarchal Narratives, Abraham, Isaac and Jacob take wives in relationships that are, according to Leviticus, incestuous (Lev. 18:9–18), since the women they take are close relatives. Sarah, Abraham's wife, is also his sister (Gen. 20:12). Isaac marries Rebekah, whose grandfather is Abraham's brother (24:3–4, 15, 24, 40), and Jacob marries Rachel, who is a daughter of Laban who is Rebekah's brother (28:1-2; 29:9-14). Indeed, Isaac and Jacob are explicitly told by their parents to marry from within their kin (Gen. 24:4, 28:1–2). Esau, Jacob's brother, does not, and attracts condemnation (26:34; 27:46). But the marriage relationships of Abraham, Isaac and Jacob are incestuous according to Leviticus 18:9–18. So according to Leviticus the patriarchs behave in an immoral way. Why should this be? Because the narratives serve the structural requirement of encouraging Israelite endogamy – one marries within the Israelite 'gene pool', and at this prototypical phase of Israel's existence this can only be achieved by marrying incestuously within the family. These stories are there to rein- force the underlying structure of Israelite identity (i.e., there is no possibility of mediation or transformation of Israel and non-Israel) as it is expressed in marriage relationships. But incest is not a model of behaviour to follow, and the story needs to be read in a rather careful and subtle way to avoid this implication. Depiction of incest serves a structural level requirement in the narrative, and it is at this level that it finds significance – i.e., incest here reinforces marriage within the group rather than being a practice to copy in itself.

So in the case of Joshua, might it be the case that the *herem* is a narrative feature that really functions to serve structural (or perhaps literary) requirements in a way that might be loosely comparable with incest in the Patriarchal Narratives? In other words, is *herem* something that is required (at the structural level perhaps) to 'make the story work' in the service of Israel- ite identity-construction? What I mean is this: The 'extreme' *herem* of Jericho in Joshua 6 is well known as unusually severe – everyone is to be killed, the city is to be destroyed, and no plunder is to be taken, except perhaps into the treasury of the Lord. But the *herem* of Jericho represents the culmination of Rahab's story and the introduction of Achan's story. Without the extreme *herem* of Jericho Rahab might have lived anyway, and Achan would not have been guilty of a crime (i.e., taking some of the *herem*), a crime that is central to his story in Joshua

7 – 8. In other words, the extreme *herem* of Jericho is required to make the story work (i.e., the extreme *herem* serves a literary function) in such a way that searching questions of Israelite identity can be posed and resolved, as we shall see (i.e., the extreme *herem* serves a structural function). So the extreme *herem* really serves literary and structural requirements – it need not be descriptive of actual practice. Thus the extreme *herem* of Jericho need not be understood in the sense of it being a historical report of an actual command and practice, and need not be understood as an expression of ancient Israelite ethics, at least in the 'plain sense'.

So, to return to the question I introduced above regarding how *herem* ought to be enacted, we can see how complicated a question this is, although perhaps we have caught a glimpse of how neo-structuralism might be a helpful tool in answering this question. We shall return to this pressing issue (and indeed to the question of whether the 'enactment of *herem*' is the right question to ask in the first place for a Christian reader of Joshua) in chapters 4 and 5 once we have studied the text of Joshua in more detail.

### Joshua and the construction of Christian identity

I alluded earlier to the 'surplus of meaning' in symbols, and used the example of the symbolism of the land in Joshua, considering the way that it developed to acquire a more obvious eschatological sense. Symbols and myths do not have static meaning and significance, and it is perhaps structuralist approaches to myth that most highlight their dynamic nature. The significance of myths is understood primarily in terms of their function and use in combination with other myths in a given context, with the importance of the 'original meaning' of a myth often receding with time. In other words, as a text like Joshua is read together with new myths it is seen in a different light – new questions are posed of the text and the text in turn poses new questions itself. So, in the case of the use of Joshua, whilst Rahab's story may relate to the construction of Israel's identity in its original context, the story is taken up into the Christian context and used in the construction of Christian identity – Rahab is an exemplar of faith, for example. But the idea of 'faith' in the Christian sense of the term is not present in Joshua as originally composed and understood, even though it might offer a good perspective with which to interpret Rahab's story in this later context, being something that is latent in the text. In other words, the myth is 'living' and speaks in new ways in new contexts, taking on new significance, perhaps often in rather complicated ways as was hinted at above, and will be explored further in chapter 5. And this dynamic understanding of the symbolism of myth is, perhaps, a good way of understanding what is going on in the allegorical interpretation of the early church – important myths are dovetailed with other 'myths' in a new context so that they continue to speak intelligibly in the shaping of identity. Thus Rahab's story can now be used to say something about Christian identity.

## Joshua as revelatory Scripture

But is this 'dynamic approach' to interpretation a problem in terms of understanding a myth (such as Joshua) as 'revelatory' Christian Scripture? In other words, must 'revelation' be understood as something that occurs only at a given moment, such as in the composing of the text, suggesting that it is what the text 'originally meant' that is of utmost importance? I don't think so. For if God's engagement with the world, through the Holy Spirit, is dynamic and relational in character, then it is entirely appropriate to see ancient texts as being brought alive to speak in new revelatory ways in new contexts through the Spirit. When fresh questions are brought to the text it will speak in fresh ways. What counts is the discernment in the Holy Spirit of what it means to use a text well as Christians. Or, to put it another way, to draw upon the work of Paul Ricoeur, a story such as Joshua is a narrative that presents a 'world of the text' that one creatively and imaginatively uses to shape the way in which one engages with the real experienced world.[12] As with any picture, this picture looks different depending on its background – on the context that it is interpreted in. However, the text itself is an act of discourse – it 'says something about something' – and so it cannot be used any old how if it is to be used *well*. Interpretation is not simply a case of asserting that 'this is what the text means for me' as if the arbiter of good interpretation is 'whatever suits me'. But the point is also that the significance of a text is not bound solely to what it 'originally meant', for as the world of the text confronts new contexts some aspects of the text can be seen in a new light, just as the text encourages the new context to be seen in a new light – a dialogue between text and new context takes place. Meanings that might have been only latent in the text may come to the fore – like the idea of faith in Rahab's story. In other words, a text like Joshua has a 'plenitude' of possible ways of being read in ever new contexts (so Rahab *could* be seen as exemplifying a traitor when read in a Canaanite context). But there is a sense in which each way of reading ought to be 'fitting' – in tune with what the text was 'seeking' to achieve as discourse.[13] Thus seeing the significance of Rahab in terms of her being a traitor fails to be a good reading because such an interpretation does violence to the text as discourse. The context with which the interpreter enters the story is important. In other words, discernment is needed to read a text like Joshua well in new circumstances. And every time we read or re-read a text we are reading it in new circumstances – we probably read Joshua differently after 9/11 for example, in that there are things that we must take into account in our reading that we did not previously.

Beyond the text of Joshua itself, for the Christian reader of Joshua however, it is first and foremost the canon of Scripture that provides guidance for the 'plenitude' and 'fittingness' of interpretation of Joshua – reading Joshua in juxtaposition with other texts in the canon simultaneously opens up new ways of reading the text well whilst closing down other possible ways of reading it. The canon both expands and limits the ways in which Joshua can be read.

## How do we know it's true?

Before ending our study of myth, there is one issue that must be dealt with. Anthropological analysis of myth is concerned

with the study of how in fact myths function in shaping societies. It is not really concerned with addressing the question of
whether such myths are in any sense 'true' or 'good'. But as
Christian readers of Scripture we will want to know more than
this – we will want to know if Joshua is 'true', or at least if it is
a *good* text to use to shape Christian identity. But there are difficulties here with what we mean by 'true'. Modernity told us
that for a 'history-like' narrative to be 'true' it must correspond
to what actually happened, with fictional narratives being
'untrue'. But in an important essay, 'The Narrative Function',
Paul Ricoeur demonstrates that things are not so simple.
Whilst history and fiction do differ, the line between them is
not as hard and fast as we might imagine. Historical narratives
require actual events to be *interpreted to connect them into a
story*, and fictional narratives are based on our *actual experience
of the world*. Good fiction is able to capture and express, often
very powerfully, insights into various aspects of living the
human life. He argues that

> both history and fiction refer to human action, although they do
> so on the basis of two different referential claims. Only history
> may articulate its referential claim in compliance with rules of
> evidence common to the whole body of science. In the conven-
> tional sense attached to the term 'truth' by the acquaintance
> with this body of science, only historical knowledge may enun-
> ciate its referential claim as a 'truth'-claim. But the very meaning
> of this truth-claim is itself measured by the limiting network
> which rules conventional descriptions of the world. This is why
> fictional narratives may assert a referential claim of another
> kind, appropriate to the split reference of poetic discourse. This
> referential claim is nothing other than the claim to redescribe
> reality according to the symbolic structures of the fiction. And
> the question, then, is to wonder whether in another sense of the
> words 'true' and 'truth,' history and fiction may be said to be
> equally 'true,' although in ways as different as their referential
> claims.[14]

Describing a narrative as 'fiction' (or 'myth') is not to say that
it is 'untrue', rather that it may refer to what is true but in a

different kind of way. In other words, returning to Origen, if a narrative has historical and ethical 'stumbling blocks', then these are cues to us to seek the 'referential claim' of a narrative somewhere other than at the historical or literal level. Or, to put it differently, the narrative is not to be judged in historical or ethical terms. We are back to the question of genre.

But then for a fictional or mythical narrative – that might or might not have historical elements – how do we know if it is 'true' even in Ricoeur's sense? Or, perhaps to put the question in a different and perhaps more helpful way, if a narrative such as Joshua is 'fictional', how do we know if we can *trust* it to be a narrative that we want to use to shape our understanding of God and our response to him? Part of the problem is that modernity has encouraged us to put too much weight on the idea of 'history' as governing what is true or trustworthy. But as W.T. Stevenson suggests,

> what is commonly termed 'history' is a mythic perception of reality. When one stands within this myth, all reality is seen as being historical in nature . . . No more damning criticism can be made of anyone than that of having falsified history, i.e. of having tampered with the 'true' and the 'sacred' . . . Consequently, I believe that what is often called 'historical con-sciousness' conforms essentially to what Eliade calls 'myth,' and hence I believe that we are justified in asserting that history is a mythic way of viewing reality.[15]

In other words, the whole notion that 'historical' implies 'truthful' is itself a mythical idea and understanding of the world!

So how then can we know the truth – and know that we know the truth? Returning to Paul Ricoeur, Ricoeur develops the ideas of 'manifestation' and 'testimony'.[16] We are able to discern what is trustworthy in view of the testimony of the reception and use of narratives – their fruits if you like (cf. Matt. 7:16) – in the formation of Christian identity especially when viewed through the ultimate manifestation of God in the person of Jesus whom we trust in faith to make God known to us. In other words, the very fact that narratives such as Joshua have been received and used as canonical points us towards accepting them as trustworthy in the formation of Christian identity. Much of the process of discernment has already been carried out. Whilst today in a scientific, critical and suspicious age we crave the necessity of verification through history or reason centred on the supposed objective abilities of the interpreting human subject, an acceptance in response to manifestation and testimony in faith would seem to be the more traditionally Christian route to pursue.

However, it might be the case that some Old Testament narratives lose significance for the construction of Christian identity, even if they have been important in a 'revelatory' sense of getting the community of God's people to where we are (for example, as with the Mosaic Law – a tutor to bring us to Christ (Gal. 3:15–25)). But the way that the loss of particular forms of significance of certain narratives might be worked out requires discernment through the guidance of the Spirit in specific cases.[17]

Finally, I think that it is helpful to compare the idea of narratives such as Joshua as having a fictional or mythical dimension to the idea of prophetic inspiration and imagination. Rather than taking historical narratives as the point of comparison for texts like Joshua, it is probably better to take prophetic narratives as the point of comparison – for they call us to shape or reshape our lives in response to God by inhabiting a prophetic 'world of the text' that has its roots in the everyday world whilst going beyond it in redescription. Indeed, it is noteworthy that in the Jewish ordering of the Old Testament (the Hebrew Bible), the book of Joshua is designated as one of the prophetic books.

In conclusion then, and to bring us back to the concerns of chapter 1, it seems that contemporary anthropological approaches to myth do indeed help to illuminate the kind of material that Joshua is, and where we might discover its significance – how it speaks to us as the word of God. In chapter 1 we saw that historical and ethical difficulties in narratives such as Joshua prompted the Church Fathers to seek the significance of Joshua in a 'spiritual sense'. Today we can see how such difficulties prompt us to seek the significance of Joshua in what we would call a symbolic sense, but a sense that is of spiritual and theological significance, and a sense that when rightly understood might look not unlike the spiritual sense of the Fathers. But what I am suggesting is not simply that Joshua needs to be understood in a more symbolic or metaphorical sense over time, but rather that it was *always* to be understood in a symbolic way, with this being related to its function as discourse. This is simply to clarify Joshua's genre.

# 3.

# Clearing the Ground: Understanding Joshua as an Ancient Text

We saw in chapter 2 that the significance of the book of Joshua is not restricted to what it might have 'originally meant'. To read it as a 'revelatory text' – as Christian Scripture – means that the text is used in ways that go beyond what it 'originally meant', such as in the case of Rahab's story. The 'world of the text' portrayed in Joshua has a 'plenitude' of meanings, meanings evoked as it is read in new situations and contexts. But this is *not* to say that we can use it as we please if we are to use it *well* to speak of God, and of our response to God, as a text that is revelatory. I suggested that a text such as Joshua ought to be used in a way that is 'fitting' to its character as discourse (being a text that is 'about something'), which means that its original concerns are not unimportant in considering how the text might be read well in any context. We need to understand the kind of world that it portrays through understanding the language, and literary conventions with respect to which it was composed, for example. Understanding Joshua's original concerns and achievements is an important preliminary stage of interpretation before going on to reading Joshua in the light of the canon of Christian Scripture, a 'canonical' way of reading that shows us how the plenitude of the text may be explored in fitting ways in the Christian context. So in this chapter I wish to develop the question of what we need to consider as background issues for reading Joshua well as discourse, and thus begin to consider the question of what it means to read Joshua in a way that is 'fitting' to its nature as discourse. Then in chapter 4 we shall look at the details of how Joshua is read as discourse in an Old Testament context before looking in chapter 5 at how the text reads in a Christian context.

Fortunately, we do not need to establish a *precise* context for Joshua's composition nor do we need to understand exactly how it was used originally in order to use it well today. Nevertheless, we cannot disregard the kind of way that it would have been heard, and the kind of material that it represents either. In other words, we need to have *sufficient* knowledge of the way in which Joshua might have been heard in ancient Israel in order to allow us to discern how we might hear Joshua well today. We have made some progress with this already. Our study of myth in chapter 2 has gone a long way towards helping us to understand what sort of material Joshua is – its genre if you like. Intellectual trends in modernity in particular have inclined readers to assume that Joshua is of the genre of 'history' (as that term is understood within modernity). The result has been that Joshua is misread in these terms and judged accordingly. But we have seen in chapter 2 that this is probably mistaken – the overly rationalistic philosophy of modernity has been foisted onto the Church and the Christian faith, with the result that stories such as Joshua are misread.[1] Reading Joshua in terms of history is not a fitting way of reading it with regard to what it represents as discourse. We must now fill in some more background details.

## The composition of Joshua

We have so far spoken of the book of Joshua as a single entity – which it now is. However, on closer inspection we see that it is made up of three main sections. Joshua 1–12 describes the conquest of the land, Joshua 13–22 describes the settlement of the land, and Joshua 23–24 provide an exhortation to Israel based on Joshua 13–22. The sections serve different functions within the book. But what is interesting is that Joshua 1–12 is largely based around the concerns of the book of

Deuteronomy, whilst Joshua 13–22 is based mainly upon the more 'priestly' concerns associated with parts of the book of Numbers,[2] whilst Joshua 23–24 is based again on concerns of the book of Deuteronomy and other ancient material.[3]

Indeed, if one analyses the language and concerns of Joshua 1–12 it may be said to be 'deuteronomistic' – i.e., derived from the book of Deuteronomy, indicated by phrases such as 'not turning to the right or to the left' in obeying the law (Josh. 1:7), phrases which are characteristic of the 'deuteronomistic' tradition.[4] Moreover, many of the stories of Joshua 1–12 have Deuteronomy in mind. The repeated 'utter destruction' (*herem*) of the inhabitants of the land throughout Joshua 1–12 stems from Deuteronomy 7:1–5, and Joshua is, in some sense, presented as a fulfilment of Deuteronomy 7:1–5. In particular, Rahab's story (Josh. 2 and 6), in which a covenant is made with her by Israel, seems to allude (ominously!) to this text. Achan's story (Josh. 7), in which Achan takes some of the plunder of Jericho, possibly has Deuteronomy 7:25–26 in view, but the blotting out of his name by the execution of him and his children has Deuteronomy 29:19–21 in view. The building of the altar (Josh. 8:30–35) reflects Deuteronomy 27:1–8, and the story of the Gibeonites, who trick Israel into making a covenant with them by pretending that they are from afar reflects Deuteronomy 20:15–17, concerning rules for warfare against those who live a long way away. And other allusions can be traced. But Joshua 1–12 really centres upon Deuteronomy 7:1–5 and the application of the *herem*, and it is worth pointing out here that the *herem* in Joshua has this very 'deuteronomistic' sense. It is used elsewhere in the Old Testament (although rather rarely) in slightly different ways, as we shall see. But the main point here is that in order to read Joshua 1–12 well it needs to be read with the concerns of Deuteronomy in view, and the concerns of deuteronomistic theology.

Turning to Joshua 13–22, deuteronomistic concerns drop out of the picture. Instead we find priestly concerns. For example, the question of the 'uncleanness' of the land across the Jordan is raised in Joshua 22:19, and the distribution of the land by lot (e.g. Josh 18:6) reflects priestly concerns. And various stories in

Joshua 13–22 reflect stories from the book of Numbers (which contains large amounts of 'priestly' material). For example, the account of the inheritance of Zelophehad's daughters (Josh. 17:3–4) reflects Numbers 36. In other words then, to read Joshua 13–22 well it should be read in priestly perspective, according to priestly theology.

Finally, we have a return to deuteronomistic materials in Joshua 23 (and perhaps Josh. 24), with a call for Israel to respond in Joshua 23 and in Joshua 24. Joshua 23 clearly has the themes of Deuteronomy 7:1–5 central to it, but interestingly there is no mention of *herem* any longer – rather, the instruction given is to avoid covenants and intermarriage. This is a crucial point, and we shall return to it later.

But is deuteronomistic theology different from priestly theology? Well, whilst there is much in common, there are important differences in emphasis. For example, in the priestly materials the ark essentially represents the presence of God, whereas in the deuteronomistic materials the ark is emphasised as holding the tablets of the law. Likewise deuteronomistic theology shows less interest in creation than priestly theology. Genesis 1:1–2:4a is regarded by most scholars as the priestly account of creation, an account that culminates in the Sabbath. This concern is reflected in the Ten Commandments as told in Exodus where the observance of the Sabbath is 'grounded' in creation (Exod. 20:8–11) – a priestly concern reflecting the priestly creation narrative. However, in the Ten Commandments as told in Deuteronomy the observance of the Sabbath is grounded in the rememberance of Israel's slavery in Egypt and Yahweh's deliverance of Israel from this slavery (Deut. 5:12–15) – there is no mention of creation here in Deuteronomy. So although these theological traditions share much in common, relating to the worship of Yahweh, there are important differences in emphasis that are important to bear in mind for reading stories that are written within these traditions.

Consideration of the composition of Joshua tells us something about how to read its various sections well as discourse – some sections are read well with deuteronomistic concerns in view, whereas other sections are read well with priestly

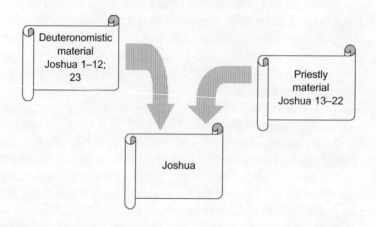

concerns in view. However, to read the book like this can risk
splitting it up in a way that reverses what is achieved in its
composition, for we have a unified book that is to be read as a
whole. But, what its composition also suggests is that in all
Figure 4: The Composition of Joshua likelihood it was originally something like two books that were important for two
different traditions in Israel's history, perhaps in rather different ways. However, at some point these two books were
combined into the one book – Joshua, the book that we now
have. Perhaps by uniting the two strands of material in one
book we are invited to read the deuteronomistic sections in
priestly terms and vice versa, something that represents an
exploration of the plenitude of the original stories. We shall see
what this looks like in practice in the next chapter. But this
growth of the book is also testimony to its mythical character
in the sense that Joshua is a 'living' text that was used and
developed over time to be an ever-new resource for the shaping of Israel's existence in response to God's continual manifestation in her midst. And this is clear on a smaller scale within the book itself, as it would seem that the various boundary
lists in Joshua 13–22 were the subject of continual updating to
suit new situations.[5]

This tells us about Joshua's composition in general terms, and
also about how difficult it is to speak of what Joshua 'originally

meant'. But I would now like to turn to consider a more specific question regarding the nature and genre of Joshua – the question of whether the book of Joshua is a 'conquest account'.

## Is Joshua a 'conquest account'?

Over the last couple of hundred years a number of inscriptions from the ancient Near East have been discovered that describe campaigns of conquest that occurred in the same period in which the Old Testament was composed. So it might be suggested that there is such a thing as an ancient Near Eastern genre of 'conquest account'. If there is such a genre, and if Joshua can be shown to share this genre, then it might tell us something about how to read Joshua well. The main study of Joshua in the light of such texts is that of K. Lawson Younger, in which Joshua 9–12 is compared with a variety of accounts of conquest.[6] To take an example, in the Assyrian *Annals of Tiglath-Pileser I* we read:

> With my valorous onslaught I went a second time to the land of Kadmuhu.
> I conquered all their cities.
> I carried off without number their booty, possessions, and property.
> I burned, razed [and] destroyed their cities.
> Now the remainder of their troops, which had taken fright at my fierce weapons and had been cowed by my strong and belligerent attack, in order to save their lives took to secure heights in rough mountainous terrain.
> I climbed up after them to the peaks of high mountains and perilous mountain ledges where a man could not walk. They waged war, combat, and battle with me; [and] I inflicted a decisive defeat on them.
> I piled up the corpses of their warriors on mountain ledges like the Inundator [i.e. Adad].
> I made their blood flow into the hollows and plains of the mountains.
> I bro[ught do]wn their booty, possessions and property from the secure heights of the mountains.

> [Thus] I ruled over the entire land of Kadmuhu; and I annexed
> [it] to the borders of my land.[7]

This is the kind of account with which Joshua is often compared, and seen as a witness to barbaric and primitive warfare,
often warranted by appeal to the will of some deity – the 'God
delusion' perhaps.

But whilst there are some obvious similarities, there are vital
differences. Younger's study concentrates on Joshua 9–1 2, but
this is not the book of Joshua. Joshua contains the stories of
Rahab and Achan for example; stories that have no parallel
elsewhere in other conquest accounts. Indeed, a good deal of
space is given to these (and other) stories in Joshua that have
little to do with the report of bloodshed. This is unlike the
extract regarding Tiglath-Pileser I that we have above, an
account that makes a good deal of the gory details. Moreover,
other conquest accounts are generally told using the first person, to bolster the image of the conquering king – 'I conquered
. . .' Again, we do not have this in Joshua, suggesting that
Joshua serves an altogether different purpose. Thus it seems
that there are crucial differences that would suggest that
Joshua does not, in fact, share this genre of 'conquest account'.

However, that said, perhaps we can learn something from a
little comparison. For example, several motifs that occur in
Joshua 10 reflect Sargon's *Letter to God*:

> Metatti, [the ruler] of Zikirtu, together with the kings of his
> neighboring regions I felled their assembly [of troops]. And I
> broke up their organized ranks. I brought about the defeat of
> the armies of Urartu, the wicked enemy, together with its allies.
> In the midst of Mt. Uauš he came to a stop. I filled the moun-
> tain ravines and wadis with their horses. And they, like ants in
> straits, squeezed through narrow paths. In the heat of my
> mighty weapons I climbed up after him; *and I filled ascents and
> descents with the bodies of [their] fighters. Over six 'double hours' of
> ground from Mt. Uauš to Mt. Zimur, the jasper mountain, I pursued
> them at the point of the javelin.* The rest of the people, who had
> fled to save their lives, whom he had abandoned that *the glori-
> ous might of Aššur my lord, might be magnified, Adad,* the violent,

the son of Anu, the valiant, *uttered his loud cry against them; and with the flood cloud and hail-stones (lit. 'the stone of heaven' [NA₄ AN-e]), he totally annihilated [qatu] the remainder.* Rusa, their prince, who had transgressed against Samaš and Marduk, who had not kept sacred the oath of Aššur, the king of the gods, became afraid at the noise of my mighty weapons; and his heart palpitated like that of a partridge fleeing before the eagle. Like a man whose blood is pouring out from him, he left Turuspâ, his royal city. Like a roaming fugitive *he hid in the recesses of his mountain.* Like a woman in confinement he became bedridden. Food and water he refused in his mouth. And thus he brought a permanent illness upon himself. *I established the glorious might of Aššur my lord, for all time to come upon Urartu. I left behind a terror never to be forgotten in the future.*[8]

In particular we discover 'stones from heaven' as a 'divine weapon', and divinely induced 'terror and fear', as in Joshua 10. Thus whilst readers of Joshua 10 have often wondered about the miraculous nature of the stones from heaven, or of the sun standing still (Josh. 10:11–13), it seems that such reports are not descriptions of history but rather 'literary motifs' that reflect the way in which stories like this are often told – perhaps in the same way that many captivating children's stories have the motif of a fire breathing dragon. So again, we find pointers to the nature of the text of Joshua and what its concerns are. We might misread the text, and do bad theology, if we focus on questions about whether God can 'suspend the laws of nature' to make the sun stand still, for example.

Finally, it is crucial to observe that whilst Joshua shares reports of mass destruction with other accounts such as these, the rather 'technical' term *herem* used in Joshua is virtually unknown outside the Old Testament. So, to the understanding of *herem* we shall now turn.

## Understanding *herem*

*Herem*, the 'utter destruction' of people, animals, houses and other objects, is one of the major themes of Joshua, occurring in all the major stories of conquest in Joshua 1–12 apart from the story of the Gibeonites. The root word occurs in Rahab's story (2:10), the fall of Jericho (6:17, 18, 21), in Achan's story (7:1, 11–13, 15), in the attack on Ai (8:26), in the account of the southern campaign (10:1, 28, 35, 37, 39 and 40) and in the account of the northern campaign (11:11, 12, 20 and 21). The only other place that it occurs in Joshua is in 22:20, which is a reference back to Achan's story. As we saw earlier, the reports of *herem* relate back to Deuteronomy 7:1–5, with Joshua seemingly narrating the 'fulfilment' of Deuteronomy 7:1–5.

However, the concept of *herem* is difficult to capture well in English, as recent attempts to render the command to '*herem* Jericho' in 6:17 indicate: 'devoted for destruction' (NRSV); 'devoted' (NIV); 'under the ban' (NAS); 'set apart' (NET); 'devoted under the curse of destruction' (NJB); 'doomed to destruction' (NKJ) and 'completely destroyed as an offering' (NLT). What the renderings indicate is that the idea of *herem* involves more than simply destruction, with the idea having a somewhat mysterious air to it. There are several reasons for this. First, *herem* is said to be 'to Yahweh' in Josh 6:17. Secondly, in Deuteronomy 13:15-16 (Eng) a town that has fallen into idolatry is to be subject to *herem 'kaliyl* [to keep the Hebrew term] to Yahweh'. Now *kaliyl* is usually understood as a noun here meaning something like 'whole offering'. If this is the case, then it would appear that *herem* implies more than simply destruction, for the idea would appear to have a 'sacrificial' or 'sacral' character to it, for what is *herem* is offered to Yahweh. Thirdly, because Achan took some of the *herem* from Jericho, an action which led to the initial defeat of Israel at Ai (Josh. 7), *herem* has often been viewed as being 'contagious', again reinforcing the idea of a 'sacral' character. Fourthly, *herem* is also the term used to describe people or objects that are irrevocably 'dedicated' to God in Leviticus 27:21, 28 and 29, where it is associated with holiness (*qodesh*). This is puzzling for in Deuteronomy 7:26 what is *herem* is abominable (*toevah*) and detestable (*shaqats*), adding to the mysterious and difficult nature of the concept. Finally, in the Septuagint (LXX), the ancient Greek translation of the Old Testament, *herem* in Josh 6:17 is translated using the term *anathema*, 'cursed', leading to the KJV translation of 6:17 as 'and the city shall be accursed'. Clearly *herem* is a very difficult idea to understand. How can we try and understand it better?

One of the usual approaches to difficult issues such as this is to look for parallels in the ancient Near Eastern world. Indeed, one of the apologetic moves in relation to the genocidal campaigns of Joshua is to suggest that such methods of conquest and warfare simply reflect their context and time, and that hyperbolic (i.e., greatly exaggerated) language is used, such as we find in the conquest accounts discussed above (although the term *herem*, or equivalent, is very seldom used). 'Holy war' is taken to be a standard practice of ancient warfare, or so it might be claimed. In light of the texts that we looked at above, this does not seem unreasonable. However, what is striking is that the uses of the specific term *herem*, or equivalents, are almost non-existent outside the Old Testament. There are only two (or possibly three, depending upon the dating of one text) known references to *herem* outside the Old Testament.[9] The most important of these is in the Mesha Inscription, a 9th century BC Moabite inscription that describes how Mesha, King of Moab, takes Israelite territory. The relevant section of this important inscription reads

> I am Mesha, the son of Kemosh[-yatti] the king of Moab, the Dibonite.
> My father was king over Moab for thirty years, and I was king after my father.
> And I made this high-place for Kemosh in Karchoh,
> [. . .]
> because he has delivered me from all kings(?),
> and because he has made me look down on all my enemies.
> Omri was the king of Israel,
> and he oppressed Moab for many days,
> for Kemosh was angry with his land.
> And his son succeeded him, and he said — he too —
> "I will oppress Moab!"
> In my days did he say [so],
> but I looked down on him and on his house,
> and Israel has gone to ruin, yes, it has gone to ruin for ever!

And Omri had taken possession of the whole la[n]d of Medeba,
and he lived there (in) his days and half the days of his son,
forty years,
but Kemosh [resto]red it in my days.
And I built Baal Meon, and I made in it a water reservoir,
and I built Kiriathaim.
And the men of Gad lived in the land of Ataroth from ancient
times,
and the king of Israel built Ataroth for himself,
and I fought against the city,
and I captured it,
and I killed all the people [from] the city as a sacrifice(?) for
Kemosh and for Moab, and I brought back the fire-hearth of his
Uncle(?) from there,
and I hauled it before the face of Kemosh in Kerioth,
and I made the men of Sharon live there, as well as the men of
Maharith.
And Kemosh said to me:
"Go, take Nebo from Israel!"
And I went in the night,
and I fought against it from the break of dawn until noon,
and I took it,
and I killed [its] whole population, seven thousand male citi-
zens(?) and aliens(?), and female citizens(?) and aliens(?), and
servant girls;
*for I had put it to the ban [herem] for Ashtar Kemosh.*
And from there, I took th[e ves]sels of YHWH,
and I hauled them before the face of Kemosh.
And the king of Israel had built Jahaz,
and he stayed there during his campaigns against me,
and Kemosh drove him away before my face,
and I took two hundred men of Moab, all its division(?),
and I led it up to Jahaz.
And I have taken it in order to add it to Dibon.[10]

But there is very little reference to this concept of *herem* outside
the Old Testament. In particular, it is very interesting that in
2 Kings 19:11 *herem* is used in the reported speech of the
Assyrian king Sennacherib's message to Hezekiah, a term that

Sennacherib uses to describe what he has already done in his campaigns of conquest according to 2 Kings, and yet in the Assyrian inscriptions that we have (and we have a good number, including those of Sennacherib), the term *herem* is never used. This is significant, as we have a number of Assyrian inscriptions that relate to precisely the same events that are narrated in 2 Kings 19.

So there is strikingly little talk of *herem* outside the Old Testament, and it seems that it does not describe a common ancient practice of warfare or conquest. But perhaps even more striking is the scarcity of the term in the Old Testament, and the observation that it is used in different ways in the Old Testament. I shall now show how it is used in three different contexts in the Old Testament, none of which relate straightforwardly to describing warfare. I shall show that *herem* is used in a deuteronomistic context relating to a particular portrayal of conquest in the deuteronomistic tradition, in a priestly context relating to dedication to Yahweh in a non-militaristic sense, and a prophetic context relating to future judgment.

*Herem* is hardly ever used to describe warfare in the books of Judges (apart from where Judges overlaps with Joshua), Samuel, Kings or Chronicles. The only significant exception is in 1 Samuel 15, the story that reports Saul's rejection. We shall return to this story briefly later, but for now note that the term *herem* is not used to describe a regular practice of warfare outside Joshua in Israel's 'historical' books that repeatedly describe wars. In other words, *herem* in the sense adopted in Deuteronomy and Joshua appears more as something relating to Israel's prototypical past than to her ongoing history and life. Indeed, *herem* is a term that is never used in the psalms.

Perhaps the major use of the idea of *herem* in the Old Testament outside Deuteronomy and Joshua is reflected in Lev 27:21, 28–29, as we noted above, where it is associated with dedication to Yahweh. But it has been commonplace to associate some of the priestly conceptions of *herem* as found here in Leviticus, together with more general priestly ideas, with the *herem* in Joshua and Deuteronomy. However, it is important to distinguish the priestly use of *herem* here in Leviticus from its deuteronomistic usage in Deuteronomy and Joshua. *Herem* seems to be used to refer to something different in these different traditions. Can this be clarified? We have already suggested that the description of *herem* in Leviticus in terms of holiness (Lev. 27:28–29) stands in some tension with its association with 'being detestable' in Deuteronomy 7:26. However, we have also seen that *herem* is said to be 'to Yahweh' (e.g. Josh. 6:17), thus resembling the vocabulary of offerings, and indeed in Deuteronomy 13:15–16 (Eng) *herem* seems to be described as a *kaliyl*, an offering. Does this in fact indicate a priestly sense to *herem* in Deuteronomy? Well, it is equally possible to translate 'to Yahweh' as 'for or on behalf of Yahweh'[11] and so perhaps there is no sacrificial sense implied. But what about Deuteronomy 13:15–16? The word *kaliyl* in fact has two senses in the Old Testament. It can either function as a noun in the sense of an offering, as it is usually taken to be in Deuteronomy 13:15–16, or it can function as an adverb to indicate completeness. This second sense is in fact the more common sense of the term in the Old Testament, and it is quite natural to read it in this way in Deuteronomy 13:15–16. It is only the assumed 'sacrificial' connotation of *herem* that has led to the usual translation of *kaliyl* as 'offering' in Deuteronomy 13. So, rather than the NRSV's rendering of Deuteronomy 13:16 as

> All of its spoil you shall gather into its public square; then burn the town and all its spoil with fire, *as a whole burnt offering* (*kaliyl*) to the LORD your God. It shall remain a perpetual ruin, never to be rebuilt.,

I suggest that Deuteronomy 13:16 ought to be read,

> All of its spoil you shall gather into its public square; then burn the town and all its spoil with fire *completely* (*kaliyl*) for the LORD your God. It shall remain a perpetual ruin, never to be rebuilt.

Finally, in relation to priestly ideas, it is common to treat *herem* as being understood to be a 'contagion' in the priestly sort of sense of the term, rather like 'uncleanness'. Indeed, it would seem that Joshua 7 expresses this idea, for it would appear that the camp of Israel has been 'contaminated' with the *herem* that Achan took, and that Israel is now facing destruction itself, having 'become *herem'*.[12] But to say that Israel has become subject to *herem*, or has been contaminated with it rather like a bacterial infection is to go beyond what the text says. We shall consider just what is going on here in Joshua 7 in the next chapter, but for now I simply wish to note that Joshua 7 need not be understood as implying that *herem* is a contagion. Indeed, when one looks at the way that *herem* is talked about in the Old Testament, it is not talked about using the same sort of vocabulary as is used to talk about other ideas that do relate to contagion or impurity in Leviticus. And it is not talked about in a conceptually equivalent way in Deuteronomy or Joshua either, apart perhaps from the ambiguous Joshua 7. But I shall argue in the next chapter that it is not the contagiousness of *herem* that is in view here. Rather, Joshua 7 is concerned with disobedience to God, and its effects, in a symbolic way. It is disobedience that is 'conatagious' and not *herem*. In summary then, it would appear that the concept of *herem* in the Old Testament has been misunderstood by reading the priestly and deuteronomistic conceptions of *herem* into each other – i.e., interpreters have assumed that Leviticus and Deuteronomy are basically talking about the same thing, when in fact they are not.[13] Perhaps the only difficulty with this assertion is the references to the *herem* of Jericho being taken to the 'treasury of the Lord' in Joshua 6:19 and 24, for this would seem to support the priestly understanding of *herem*. But these two verses are widely taken to be later additions to the text of Joshua – the reference to the treasury is anachronistic (i.e., out of place in the narrative world), and, the idea of *herem* as detestable in Deuteronomy 7:26 does not sit well with bringing it into the treasury! In other words, the tradition for reading priestly and deuteronomistic understandings of *herem* together began very early, and is something that can be seen as developing further in a re-telling of Joshua in the Dead Sea Scrolls text 4Q379 where Joshua 7 is explicitly linked with Leviticus 27:21, 28–29.[14] In other words, to read Joshua 6–7 well it is important to read it against its deuteronomistic background, rather than a priestly one, as we saw in the first section of this chapter, for this is how it is read in a fitting way. There are problems when one tries to merge the priestly and deuterono-mistic conceptions of *herem*.

Turning to the prophetic materials, *herem* is sometimes used to narrate what will happen in the future, either to Israel or to the nations, in the context of a prophetic warning or encour-agement to Israel (e.g. Jer. 51:1–3). But when such threatened judgment did occur, it was never narrated as occurring as being through a practice of *herem*. In other words, one might say that in Deuteronomy and Joshua *herem* is a concept of Israel's prototypical past, whilst in the prophetic materials it is a concept of the future. *Herem*, when associated with warfare or genocide, never seems to describe an actual practice of Israel in the present – *it is 'never now' in terms of its literal appli-cation. It only has a 'literal existence' in the world of the text, either of the past or the future but 'never now'*. In other words, it seems to have a mythical or symbolic character that we shall con-sider below.

Moreover, there is very little mention of *herem* in the Pentateuch (i.e., the first five books of the Old Testament) in the context of warfare and conquest. It is only really in Deuteronomy that we find much reference to *herem*. But what is important here is that if Deuteronomy 7:1–5 presents us with one command or 'portrait' of how Israel is to enter into the promised land, the Pentateuch presents two others, shown in Exodus 23:23 and Leviticus 18:25, 28 and 20:22–26. In Exodus 23:23 it is said that the local inhabitants of the land will 'van-ish' (*kahad*, but note that English translations sometimes tend to translate this verse in accordance with Deut. 7:2), whereas in Leviticus the land is said to 'vomit out' (*qy'*) the locals. In other words, three different traditions in the Pentateuch provide three different portraits or interpretations of how space will be made available in the promised land for Israel. This would again suggest caution in seeing *herem* as reflecting a historical description of Israel's entrance to the land.

Furthermore, returning to Deuteronomy specifically, in its context in Deuteronomy 7:1–5 there are problems with under-standing the *herem* command in 7:1–2 as something literally commanded that was to be fulfilled or practiced 'literally'. Deut 7:2–3 prohibits Israel's making of covenants with locals and intermarriage with locals. But if the locals were destroyed as per 7:2, there would be no need for this command – corpses do not provide temptations to intermarry! This might suggest then that *herem* has a more 'rhetorical' symbolic sense in Deuteronomy 7:1–2, at least in the way that the text is to be applied or enacted (to use Victor Turner's term from the previous chapter). What might this sense be then? There are two texts that give us some clues outside Deuteronomy. Those are Joshua 23 and Ezra 9:1–2. We shall study Joshua 23 in the next chapter, but to take Ezra 9:1-2, this text, reporting Israel's failure to keep herself separate from others, has clear resonances with Deuteronomy 7:1–5, and it is often thought to be dependent upon it. But there is no reference to *herem* in Ezra 9:1–2. Rather, what Israel is said to have failed to do is that she has not separated herself (*badal*) from the locals. And this sense of separation is implied in Deuteronomy 7:1–5 and in Joshua 23, for Israel is to make no covenants with the locals, and is not to intermarry with them. In Deuteronomy and Joshua this is because the locals will lead Israel astray into the worship of other gods and into idolatry. So it seems possible at least that *herem* in Deuteronomy 7:1–5 has a rhetorical function, i.e. to urge the separation of Israel from 'non-Israel' in an existentially provocative way to portray the ideal of the separation of Israel from non-Israel. To return to the language of neo-structuralism, *herem* is then a fine example of the expression of non-mediation and non-transformation between Israel and non-Israel. *Herem* flatly denies the possibility of mediation and transformation between Israel and non-Israel, expressed using the idea of annihilation *in the world of the text,* an idea that carries across to enactment in the real world in terms of separation. In other words, *death and destruction are the ultimate symbolic expressions of separation.* For Ezra 9:1–2 and Joshua 23 this is all well and good. But what about Joshua 1–12, a text that seems to report the fulfilment of Deut 7:1-2? We must now turn to a careful reading of Joshua, bearing in mind what we have learned about *herem* so as to read the text in a 'fitting' way as mythical discourse.

## Summary

Before doing so, let us summarize briefly where we have got to in this chapter. First, we have seen that Joshua is the product of the fusion of two traditions, a priestly one and a deuteronomistic one. This observation has bearings upon what it means to read Joshua well, as we have seen with *herem*. Secondly, we have seen that the book of Joshua is not really a 'conquest account'. It may have the appearance of one, which might be for rhetorical purposes, to make it a captivating story that people will pay attention to, but it is not a conquest account. However, the use of certain themes in other ancient texts indicates that similar themes may be used in Joshua, such as 'stones from heaven' as a divine weapon, which tells us something about the nature of the text. In other words, some of the descriptions in Joshua are not of 'history' but are common 'literary devices' used in the telling of stories like this, rather like the fire-breathing dragon in other types of literature. Finally, our investigation of *herem* revealed that whilst *herem* is clearly a key term in Joshua, it is a rare term elsewhere. It is virtually unknown in the ancient world outside the Old Testament, and it is rare in the Old Testament. It seems to be used in three types of literature in the Old Testament in significantly different ways – in a deuteronomistic sense, as in Deuteronomy 7:1–5, in a priestly sense, as in Leviticus 27:21, 28–29, and in a prophetic sense, as in Jeremiah 51:1–3.

| | *Herem* | | |
|---|---|---|---|
| **Tradition** | Priestly | Deuteronomistic | Prophetic |
| **Key texts** | Lev 27:21, 28-29 | Deut 7:1-5, 25-26 | Jer 51:1-3 |
| **Meaning** | Evokes the idea of irrevokable separation *to* God – *herem* is holy | Evokes the idea of separation *from* idolatry using the image of past annihilation – *herem* is detestable | Develops the image of annihilation as the future fate of those who disregard God to evoke a response to God in the present |

*Herem* is a strong expression of non-mediation, but in different ways being used symbolically to evoke different sorts of response to God.

**Table 1: *Herem* in the Old Testament**

Importantly though, *herem* does not describe a practice of actual warfare – it is a term of the past or of the future when used in the non-priestly sense. It is also a term used in only one of three pictures of Israel's entrance to the land, and in the one in which it occurs, Deuteronomy 7:1–5, it seems to have more of a symbolic, rhetorical function than the function of a literal command. Together, these observations suggest that *herem* is a properly 'mythical' or symbolic concept with a somewhat 'opaque', 'second-order' significance relating to separation. It is not a concept that describes or interprets a 'literal' historical practice. This brings us to Joshua. I shall now show that whilst Joshua builds upon *herem's* sense in Deuteronomy 7:1-5, it actually does something quite subtle and unexpected with the symbolic concept, and uses it in yet another way.

# 4.

# Reading Joshua

In this chapter I would like to present something of an exploration of the story of Joshua as a text in the context of the Old Testament. I am concerned with tackling the question of what Joshua is about as a piece of discourse within the world of the Old Testament. I do not intend to address the question of Joshua's Christian significance here – that will come in the next chapter where I shall consider how the plenitude of the text may be explored well in new Christian contexts as new questions are put to the text. Here, I am more concerned with establishing what it means to read Joshua in a fitting way so as to consider the kind of way in which it would have been heard as discourse written to achieve something. This chapter is not intended to be a detailed commentary on the text, but is rather a discussion of what the story is about in terms of understanding the 'big picture' of what is going on. A map is provided over the page for those who wish to follow the geographic aspects of the story, although I shall presume that the reader is familiar with the text of Joshua.

## Joshua 1–12: the conquest

### Joshua 1: Joshua commissioned

Joshua commences where Deuteronomy left off, after the death of Moses, with Joshua now being charged to lead the Israelites into the Promised Land. Joshua 1 introduces a number of

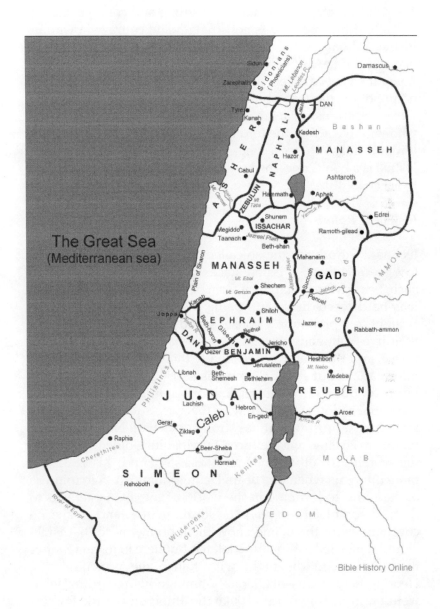

The Great Sea
(Mediterranean sea)

Bible History Online

important concerns. There is the promise of the land as gift, and of God being with Joshua like he was with Moses (1:1–5). In 1:6–9 there as an exhortation to be strong and courageous. But it is interesting that this is not strength and courage in warfare in the ordinary sense – rather, it is courage and strength in obeying the Law of Moses. Language taken from the military domain has been taken and reapplied to paint a picture of the nature of obedient responsiveness to God. Joshua 1 also introduces the 'transjordanian' tribes – that is, the tribes of Israel who will live across the Jordan on the 'wrong' side (east of the Jordan), and so we see a concern with *all* of Israel here (1:12–15). Joshua is a book concerned with a *unified* Israel, and an *obedient* Israel (1:16–18).

### Joshua 2: Rahab

Joshua 2 introduces the so-called 'spy mission' and Rahab. I say 'so-called' spy mission since although it is introduced as such, being a fairly standard form of story, on closer inspection it is hard to credit it with being a spy story. The 'spies' go straight to a prostitute's house, spend the night there, flee for their lives following the arrival of the king's agents at Rahab's house, and then return to Joshua without any useful strategic information. But it is an ominous story. It has echoes of the failed conquest of Numbers 13. More significantly, by locating the initial action at Shittim, with the spies subsequently going straight to a prostitute, it has strong links with Numbers 25. In Numbers 25 Israel was seduced by Moabite women, leading to the worship of other gods, and disaster. And this is all the more ominous when one bears Deuteronomy 7:1–5 in mind as background to Joshua – in the world of the text Israel was to destroy completely (*herem*) the locals in the land, make no covenants with them, and show them no mercy so that Israel would not be led astray into idolatry. But here in Joshua 2, after the spies spend the night with Rahab the prostitute (the Hebrew here seems deliberately ambiguous regarding what went on in the night, rather like the ambiguity of the English phrase 'spending the night with . . .') they make a covenant with her to return the 'kindness' (*hesed*) that she showed them in hiding them from the king's messengers! It is worth paying close attention to some of the details here. To start with, the first mention of *herem* in the book of Joshua occurs here in 2:10, and it is placed in the speech of Rahab. So in a sense Rahab understands what Israel is doing, and perhaps rather ironically, reminds the spies of this! Secondly, Rahab's 'confession' in 2:11 is a confession *par excellence*. The wording of the confession is matched in only two other places in the Old Testament – the confession of Moses in Deuteronomy 4:39, and the confession of Solomon in 1 Kings 8:23. Thirdly, Rahab's action is interpreted in the story as being an act of *hesed*. *Hesed* is a specific and important term in the Old Testament, often translated as 'steadfast love'. It is the word that occurs in famous key passages such as Exodus 34:6 where Yahweh proclaims his nature to Moses, and in Micah 6:8 where Yahweh recounts what he truly desires from Israel. It is also the repeated refrain of Psalm 136, and occurs in the Decalogue (the Ten Commandments) to describe what is at the heart of the covenant between Yahweh and Israel (Deut. 5:10). It is thus a loaded term associated with the relationship between Yahweh and Israel, and is a term used for the sort of response that Yahweh seeks of Israel. All this suggests that Rahab is an ambiguous character. On the one hand, she is a Canaanite and a prostitute – she is a clear example of an outsider and one to fear for she is likely to seduce Israelites into sexual immorality, something associated with the worship of other gods (cf. Num. 25). But on the other hand, she offers an exemplary confession matched only by Moses and Solomon in the Old Testament, and in her actions she is characterized as doing that which is at the heart of the covenant of Israel and Yahweh – she is characterized by the quality of life and action that is to characterize the Israelite. Remember back to chapter 2 when we looked at structuralism. Now classical structuralism identified one of the concerns of myth as resolving contradictions and tensions. It seems that Rahab is, symbolically, an example of a character that creates tension. On the one hand, she looks like the paradigmatic outsider, yet on the other hand she acts like the paradigmatic insider. How will this tension be resolved? It appears that Joshua may be concerned with precisely this sort

of issue. What will happen to Rahab and her family? Will they
be spared? Have the spies sinned in making a covenant with
Rahab? Will this lead to disaster as in Numbers 25? The narrator will keep us in suspense until Joshua 6 – a mark of good
storytelling![1]

Before moving on it is worth pausing to consider one aspect
of the story that has troubled commentators throughout the
ages. And it is this – that Rahab lied to save the spies. Should
this be seen positively or negatively? The story is not really
concerned with 'the problem of lying'. The story interprets her
actions in the most positive terms – hiding the spies is interpreted as an act of *hesed*. In other words, we should not be troubled with Rahab's deception, for the narrative interprets her
actions positively, as showing kindness or even 'steadfast love'.

### Joshua 3 – 4: crossing the Jordan

Turning now to Joshua 3 – 4, we have an extended report of the
miraculous crossing of the Jordan. The story clearly recalls the
crossing of the sea in Exodus 15 (cf. Josh. 4:23). God piles up
the waters so that Israel can cross on dry ground. But what is
the significance of this miraculous crossing? Why is it given so
much space in the story and what is it trying to tell us?
Christians are often hung up with questions of miracles and
what really happened here. Can it be given a 'naturalistic'
explanation? For example, it has been noted that the soft lime-
stone banks of the Jordan have sometimes collapsed and tem-
porarily dammed it, once as the result of an earthquake, on 11
July 1927.[2] Does an event like this lie behind the story? To seek
to rationalize the account – via appeal to a naturalistic explanation like this – or to provide an apologetic for the miraculous
event is to miss the point. These are not the concerns of the
story. Naturalistic explanations of the event employed to
defend or to explain its 'historicity' are attempts to replace the
story that we are given in the Word of God with another story
(the story of what some people might think 'really' happened).
Likewise to reject the story if a plausible naturalistic explanation cannot be found is also misguided for both theological
and/or literary reasons. If we are beginning to see that Joshua

is rich in symbolism, then might this account have symbolic significance primarily? Joshua certainly dwells on the importance of the crossing, with two whole chapters devoted to it, with reports of memorials being erected so that Israel will remember it, with the memorials being a spur to tell the story again (4:21–24). And 4:24 provides us with an interpretation of the event – that the peoples of the land might know the power of the Lord, and, crucially, that Israel might fear God. Or, in other words, so that Israel might respond appropriately to God. But how might this relate to the crossing in a symbolic sense? There are several important points to note here. The Jordan did not present a real obstacle to the entrance to the land such that a miracle of this order was required for Israel to cross. For example, it does not present an obstacle in Genesis 32:11, Joshua 2:7, 22:19, 24–25, Judges 3:28, 8:4, 10:9, 12:5 and 2 Samuel 17:22.[3] This makes the symbolic nature of the mode of crossing here, and its 'mythical' nature all the more clear – the miraculous Jordan crossing is symbolic, ideological and confessional in significance (Josh. 24:11; Ps. 66:6 and Micah 6:4–5).[4] This observation would shed some light on the concern with the 'transjordanian' tribes of Joshua 1 whose story is developed at length in Joshua 22, a story which asks the question of whether one can live 'on the wrong side' of the Jordan and still be an Israelite. So perhaps to be an Israelite is to be someone who has 'crossed' the Jordan. Indeed, the very dense use of the Hebrew word *avar*, meaning 'to cross' in Joshua 3–4 emphasises the importance of the Jordan crossing as the crossing of an important boundary. *Avar* is used 22 times in 41 verses here, and is a word that crops up a lot in Joshua. This is significant, for one of the techniques of the storytellers of the Old Testament is the use of 'keywords' to draw attention to the importance of particular themes in a story. 'Crossing' is important for Joshua (cf. 1:2). The crossing of the Jordan reflects the transition of a wandering people into a people with land, a land flowing with milk and honey, representing a change of status for the people.

The significance of *avar* is illustrated in Deut 29:11 and 30:18, and the reception and development of these texts in the Dead Sea Scrolls text the Community Rule, 1QS. This text uses *avar* to describe 'crossing into' the covenant, which is identified with 'crossing' into the community in 1QS. Indeed, 1QS i.16f reads, 'All who enter the order of the community shall cross (*avar*) into the covenant in God's presence and do all that he commanded' and W.H. Brownlee notes that the community rule contains a 'liturgy' that enacts this crossing, a 'crossing ceremony' that is associated with ceremonial washing (1QS ii.25–iii.12),[5] and suggests that

> The fact that [Deuteronomy] 29:11 indicates the intention of 'crossing into the sworn covenant' and 30:18 speaks of 'crossing the Jordan' may have led the people of Qumrân to equate the two uses of the verb '*āvar*. Symbolically one was also passing over into the land which God had promised the patriarchs by covenant. This suits the military character of the procession as depicted in the Community Rule, making of the event an annual memorial of the Conquest.[6]

Brownlee notes that the instructions for the order of the procession in the ceremony (1QS ii.19–25) evoke the instructions for the procession in Joshua. So the 'crossing' ceremony in the community is a form of 're-enactment' of the Jordan crossing in a new context, inspired by Joshua. In other words the Qumran community uses Joshua to (imaginatively) shape and interpret its existence, with Joshua 3–4 symbolizing crossing into new life, something developed in Joshua 5, drawing upon the understanding of 'crossing' in Deuteronomy 29:11 and 30:18.

So, in summary, if life in the Promised Land represents life in all its fullness for Israel, where Israel may enter into rest with Yahweh, then the crossing of the Jordan reflects the creation of and entrance into this new life. We see that the land symbolizes the fullness of life with Yahweh in covenantal relationship with him, with all its associated blessings, and that crossing the Jordan symbolizes crossing into this life. It is symbolically portrayed in spectacular terms to evoke the wonder of entering into this new life – it is a new life miraculously and graciously given by Yahweh. This is not to say that the actual land, and daily life in it, was unimportant as if the land was 'merely' a symbol, or as if to say that it was only the more abstract aspects of the symbolism that were important. Remember that symbols *embody* or *participate in* what it is that they symbolize. Daily life in the actual physical land embodies and shares in life with Yahweh in its fullness.

### Joshua 5: preparing to take the land

Now that Israel has crossed into the land, in Joshua 5, we see something of what this new life in the land involves. It is a life that involves circumcision as a symbol of the covenant,[7] it involves the remembrance of the Passover, and it involves Yahweh's provision of food from the land.[8] It is interesting to note that in the text of Joshua preserved in the Dead Sea Scrolls, a text known as 4QJosh[a], the account of the building of the altar and the writing and the reciting of the law that occurs in Joshua 8:30–35 in English translations of Joshua is actually found here in Joshua 5. This location, in Joshua 5 rather than Joshua 8, actually makes very good sense for two reasons. First, it brings together important aspects of Israel's identity – law, circumcision and Passover. But secondly, the injunction in Deuteronomy 27 to build the altar that is reflected in this account (8:30–35 in English translations), commands that the altar is to be built as soon as Israel has crossed the Jordan. So again, locating this account of the altar construction in Joshua 5 makes good sense. Thus Joshua 5:1–12 introduces the reader to something of the nature of the new life in the land that Israel will enjoy.

But what about the rather mysterious Joshua 5:13–15 where the commander of Yahweh's army appears to Joshua and refuses Joshua's question, with a response of 'no' to the question of whether the commander is for Israel or for her enemies? It is easy to misread this important little account. Perhaps the account is intended to make Israel think about her relationships with others – with outsiders – in terms that are rather more demanding than a simplistic approach that says 'God is on our side'. Whilst source critics find this account unsatisfactory as it stands and assume that a more satisfactory ending has been lost, perhaps one only finds it unsatisfactory if one assumes that the book of Joshua is essentially about conquest, and that Yahweh is firmly on the side of ethnic Israel in the conquest. But what if Joshua is actually concerned with *challenging*, or at least *qualifying*, such an exclusivist view – an exclusivist view represented in Deuteronomy 7:1–5? This is hinted at in Rahab's story – despite its ominous feel, nothing bad has happened to Israel despite the commands of Deuteronomy! Perhaps Joshua 5:13–15 encourages the reader to re-think the common perspective that there is 'us' and 'them' and that God is on 'our' (i.e., ethnic Israel's) side. Perhaps it encourages one to move beyond such categorization – more generally of appropriating the language of 'God' with regard to 'taking sides', maybe for political ends. In effect the commander of the Lord's army refuses to take sides as Joshua wishes, and refuses Joshua's question even, to make things look rather different, calling forth a response of worship from Joshua. In other words, the divine messenger encourages Israel to consider whether or not they have aligned themselves with Yahweh instead of asking whether or not Yahweh is on their side. As we shall see, this mysterious little encounter might be an important interpretative key to help us to read Joshua.

### Joshua 6: Jericho and Rahab

The story of the fall of Jericho in Joshua 6 is, perhaps, one of the best known stories in the Bible. The people process around the city for seven days with the Ark, with priests sounding horns. On the final day, seven circuits of the city are made, the people shout, and the walls fall. Israel charges into the city and subjects everything to *herem* (i.e., they destroy everyone and everything), apart from Rahab and her family who are spared in accordance with the oath in chapter 2. The story certainly captures the imagination – but what is it about? Why is the destruction so abnormally extreme (cf. Josh. 8:2)? The city of Jericho was an extremely well fortified and virtually impregnable city (Josh. 6:1). Archaeological excavations have revealed the extent of the city's fortifications. Presumably it would have been well known in tradition just what an imposing city

Jericho was, having something of a reputation. In a sense then the city might be said to symbolize the opposition that Israel is likely to encounter in taking possession of the land, with Jericho evoking the most impregnable opposition. But there is no other account quite like Joshua 6 in the Old Testament or in the ancient Near East. Whilst there are accounts that report sieges and the collapse of city walls in battle, such accounts are of a different nature. The ritual procession around Jericho transforms the idea of a military siege into an event of the ritual domain. So in Joshua 6 the focus is taken off issues of warfare and battle as such, and placed instead on issues of ritual performance, and on the rescue of Rahab. Look at how much space in the story is given to the reporting and description of warfare and destruction – very little – and compare it with the amount of space that is given to the ritual procession and to Rahab. This gives us an indication of what is of concern to the narrator here. But why should the destruction be so extreme here, and extreme even with regard to *herem*? Well, if it was not extreme then the stories of Rahab (Josh. 2) and of Achan (Josh. 7), whose story the tale of Jericho introduces, would not work. If the destruction of Jericho was not total, then Rahab might have got lucky and been one of the survivors. She might have lived through good fortune rather than as a result of the oath made. Moreover, if plunder could be taken then Achan would not be guilty of taking some of the plunder in disobedience to the command given (Josh. 6:18) – he, and many others would have been fortunate in being able to obtain great     riches from the spoils of war. There would be no story of Achan.

In many ways Achan is Rahab's foil, and their stories meet in the razing of Jericho. But before turning to Achan's story, it is worth noting that Rahab's story finds its resolution – or at least its near resolution – here. She is not explicitly said to become an Israelite, although this is implied and made concrete in later tradition in which she marries Joshua and is an ancestor of some of the prophets in the Jewish tradition, and is of course placed in Jesus' genealogy in the Christian tradition (Matt. 1:5). Rahab is spared as per the oath with the spies, an oath that Joshua confirms. However, as we have already noted, Rahab's story is ominous in the light of Deuteronomy 7:1–5 –

surely she is the very kind of person with whom no oath should be made! Moreover, there is no report in Joshua of any-one seeking Yahweh in relation to Rahab, either when the oath was made, or when Jericho was taken. Again, this places the story in a slightly ambiguous light.

But Joshua is portrayed as being wholeheartedly obedient in the book (Josh. 10:40, 11:23), with God being with him (6:27). Joshua is an unusual character in Old Testament narrative in that his portrayal is so uniformly positive. Unlike characters such as Abraham, Moses and David he seems not to have any flaws or rebellious moments. In other words, the overall uniformly posi-tive portrayal of Joshua in the book suggests that the decision to spare Rahab should be seen in a positive light. This sparing of Rahab then qualifies (although, as we shall see in Joshua 23 espe-cially, it does not reject) the ideology of Deuteronomy 7:1–5. The narrator of Joshua guides the reader to what is an ideologically difficult position. Hence the slight ambiguity. To challenge Israel's ideology in the way that I suggest that the narrator here wishes to, the narrator needs to be subtle and careful, making the reader think and ponder, rather than coming straight out with what he wants to say. This is the art of good rhetoric. And what the narrator wants to say is this – that the construction of Israel's identity reflected in Deuteronomy 7:1–5 needs adjustment. There are those outside the community of Israel who, like Rahab, seem to be way outside the community and what might seem to be Israelite, but who act and confess in a way that is thoroughly and outstandingly Israelite. In other words, despite appearances, Rahab exhibits a quality of responsiveness to Yahweh that many an Israelite can only aspire to. The narrator forces the reader to ponder the question of whether it is right that someone like this should be excluded from the community of Israel as indicated in Deuteronomy 7. This, it seems, it what Rahab's story is about.[9]

### *Joshua 7: Achan*

So, what about Achan then? Joshua 7 reports an unsuccessful attack on Ai, following which Achan is identified as the one responsible for the failure of the attack, since he kept some of the *herem* of Jericho, which brought divine wrath against Israel.

Indeed, Achan's story is intertwined with the story of the attacks on Ai (Josh. 7–8). But Ai is a name that means something like 'ruin', and so the city of Ai, 'the ruin', contrasts symbolically with the impregnable, fortified Jericho. So one would expect Israel to be able to take Ai with ease, and this expectation is reflected in the first attack on Ai, an attack that ends in disaster for Israel (Josh. 7:3–5). But what is the story really about? We are given a clue as to how to read it at the very beginning. The story is not about military tactics, or overconfidence, or even about the failure to enquire of Yahweh perhaps, even if these concerns may lurk in the background of the story. The story is primarily about Achan and his disobedience in relation to what was *herem* at Jericho, and how this affects Israel. But how does Achan's disobedience affect Israel, and what is at the heart of his disobedience?

As I suggested in the previous chapter, it has been commonplace to treat *herem* objects as a 'contagion'. Crudely speaking, the 'accursed' nature of such objects is seen as 'infecting' the whole camp in which they are located on this understanding of *herem*. So for many interpreters it is this 'infection' of the camp with *herem* objects that gives rise to Israel's defeat, and explains the story. But I suggest that this is not the right way to understand the *herem* objects, and is therefore not quite the right way to understand the story. I argued in chapter 3 that *herem* does not, in general, convey any sense of contagion. So what is it doing here in Joshua 7? In light of our reading of Joshua so far, it seems that a symbolic understanding is worth pursuing. What Achan's crime here indicates is disobedience to Yahweh, and in particular, disobedience as expressed through the idea of the covenant. Indeed, Joshua 7 interprets Achan's crime in terms of coveting, lying and stealing (7:11 and 21). This is very much the language of the Decalogue, the Ten Commandments. Using the 'concrete' picture of *herem* as a symbol, Achan is shown to be one who symbolically rebels against the covenant as expressed in the Decalogue. Achan thus symbolizes the non-Israelite as one who disregards Yahweh.

However, Achan is apparently depicted as one who is a model Israelite – his genealogy is given (7:1), and repeated for emphasis (7:16–18), establishing him as the model Israelite of the tribe of Judah. So Achan contrasts with Rahab – Rahab appears to be the model non-Israelite, being a Canaanite prostitute, but behaves just like an Israelite in terms of her 'confession' and behaviour when 'confronted' with *herem* (2:10). Achan appears as the model Israelite with an established genealogy, yet he behaves like a non-Israelite when 'confronted' with *herem* at Jericho. This association of the two characters is strengthened by the way in which the narrator carefully uses keywords in the stories. Rahab hides (*taman*, 2:6) the spies (*malakim*, 6:17) sent by Joshua leading to her rescue from Jericho, whilst Achan hides (*taman*, 7:21) the *herem*, which the messengers (*malakim*, 7:22) sent by Joshua discover, leading to his death. And just as Rahab's family are spared, Achan's children are killed to make the contrast complete, with their death marking the 'blotting out' of his name from Israel as indicated in Deuteronomy 29:19–21, a text that is much in view in Achan's story. He has become the outsider.

But why then is Achan's story intertwined with the story of Ai? Could it not just be told by itself? Telling the story in this way makes it a captivating story that will grab attention, a story full of excitement and surprise. But it does something else too. The failed attack on Ai indicates the corporate and communal results of disobedience to Yahweh, highlighting the seriousness of the problem. In a sense then it is disobedience to Yahweh that is the contagion, and not *herem*. Reading this account from a priestly perspective, as suggested in chapter 3, may highlight this idea. Joshua 7 uses the priestly term *maal*, to 'act unfaithfully' which might hint at the possibility of a priestly reading of the text, even if the story is basically one that is shaped by the deuteronomist. Indeed, we must be careful not to transpose priestly ideas about *herem* into this story.[10] But the idea of sin as contaminating the camp of Israel and causing Yahweh to withdraw his presence is something well established in the priestly tradition.[11] So reading Joshua 7 in this priestly way highlights this aspect of Achan's sin, that it leads to the withdrawal of Yahweh's presence from Israel, showing Israel's military strength to be weak and ineffective in itself.

So the seriousness of disobedience to Yahweh by one offender for the whole of Israel is evoked in Joshua 7, and thus the need for every Israelite to keep the covenant faithfully is suggested. Achan is one who brings trouble on Israel, something indicated by his name. The name Achan reflects a wordplay on the Hebrew verb *achar*, meaning 'to trouble', a word used in 6:18 to indicate what would happen to Israel if they were disobedient at Jericho. *Achar* is also the root of the name of the place Achor at the end of Joshua 7, being the place where Achan was buried. This use of wordplays indicates the literary and symbolic significance of this story, shown here in the choice of the names, guiding the way in which we read and understand the story. Achan is the one who brings trouble on Israel by being disobedient to the commands about the *herem* (Josh. 6:18). Achan is the symbolic troublemaker who disregards Yahweh by ignoring the covenant, symbolized through response to herem.

### Joshua 8: on the road again

Joshua 8 then describes a successful attack on Ai. What then of Joshua 8? It simply continues a captivating story built around conquest and indicates, in the world of the text, that the conquest will now proceed with Yahweh being 'with' Israel again after the previous unsuccessful attack, bringing closure to Achan's story. The note that Israel can keep the plunder now (8:2) highlights the way in which the extreme *herem* at Jericho functions in the story of Joshua 6.

### Joshua 9: the Gibeonites

The stories of Rahab and Achan indicate that there can be those outside Israel whose character clearly reflects that of the Israelite, and those inside Israel whose character reflects that of the outsider. Although surprising, they represent clear-cut cases of 'reversals'. But what about less clear-cut cases? The story of the Gibeonites in Joshua 9 reflects just such a less clear-cut case, but their story is another tale that is almost devoid of the reporting of, or description of warfare. The Gibeonites are introduced as responding to Israel's conquest in a different way from other local kings who conspire to fight Israel (9:1–3).

Rather than fighting Israel they attempt to trick Israel into making a treaty with them so as to spare themselves by pretending that they are not locals but rather a group from far off. The background to this story is in Deuteronomy 20, which distinguishes between locals and those from afar in terms of rules for battle in relation to the command of *herem* in Deuteronomy 7:1–5. Peace may be made with those who live far away, but not with locals. And so the Gibeonites enter into a clever deception, and seek a covenant with Israel. Much of the language of Joshua 9 reflects covenantal language, but it is noteworthy that it is explicitly said that the Israelites did not enquire of Yahweh (9:14), an ominous note that is followed by the report that Joshua made the covenant with the Gibeonites. The Gibeonite ruse is subsequently discovered, but, even after some grumbling, the Israelites are faithful to the oath sworn, even though the Gibeonites are relegated to the status of servants. The chapter closes with the note that the Gibeonites remain Israel's servants 'to this day'.

Joshua 9 is an ambiguous story in many ways. However, there is no explicit evaluation of the various actions offered. Whilst the note regarding the failure to consult Yahweh is ominous, it is in fact ambiguous. There is no negative appraisal of the events that transpire from the narrator. Nor is there any negative appraisal from Joshua or from Yahweh. Moreover, whilst we might naturally think of the deception of the Gibeonites in negative terms, seeing them as liars, this kind of behaviour and its significance is in fact culturally conditioned. In some societies deception in circumstances such as the Gibeonites were in is a praiseworthy action.[12] So rather like Rahab they need not be seen as sinning through lying. Moreover, their deception of Israel here is an ironic reversal of Israel's deception of the Hivites (= Gibeonites) in Genesis 34. In other words, the Gibeonites act in a similar way to Israel!

But their deception, their *arumah* (9:4), is a concept that is rather ambiguous in the Old Testament. It can carry positive connotations (e.g. in the book of Proverbs, such as Prov. 1:4) and negative connotations (e.g. Exod. 21:14). Thus whilst Rahab exemplifies what is arguably the most central quality that is to characterize Israel, i.e., *hesed*, and offers an exemplary confession matched only by Moses and Solomon, the Gibeonites offer a rather weak confession of fear (9:24), and display rather ambiguous characteristics that do relate to the identity of Israel, but only somewhat marginally (*arumah*, 9:4). In other words, the Gibeonites are rather 'marginal' figures who end up in a rather 'marginal' status – they are spared, and live among Israel, but as servants. So whilst Rahab and Achan reflect fairly clear-cut cases of true identity, the Gibeonites represent a more difficult, ambiguous and marginal case – they are poised on the boundary. So whilst the stories of Rahab and Achan serve to reverse expectations of who counts as an insider or outsider, the story of the Gibeonites serves to blur the actual boundary between insider and outsider. So whilst one might have thought that the author of Joshua was simply offering a different set of criteria for defining insiders and outsiders, and of who Israel might include or exclude from their community in line with Deuteronomy 7, the story of the Gibeonites seems deliberately to make problematic the whole notion of a clearly defined community boundary.

What is interesting about the story of the Gibeonites too is that there is no use of the word *herem* anywhere in their story, even though there are places that cry out for its use, such as 9:24, where the word used is the verb *shamad*, which is simply the common word for destruction. Joshua 9 is the only major story of these 'battle accounts' in Joshua that does not use the term *herem*. Perhaps then *herem* symbolizes something of a 'test' that demonstrates one's identity in relation to Israel. When confronted with *herem* Rahab acts in such a way as to reveal her character as 'true Israel', whereas when Achan is 'confronted' with *herem* he acts in such a way as to reveal that his heart is set somewhere other than with Israel and Yahweh. But this 'test' is then shown to be too crude to establish the nature of the Gibeonites – the omission of *herem* from the narrative is a subtle literary clue that suggests this. In the end, there is no simple 'test' that establishes where one's heart and identity lies in all cases – there are ambiguous borderline cases.

*Joshua 10 – 11: conflict with hostile kings*

Now, just as Joshua 9 was introduced with a note about hostile kings conspiring to fight against Israel, so Joshua 10 and 11 are introduced with reports of hostile kings conspiring to fight, against the Gibeonites in Joshua 10:1–5, and against Israel in Joshua 11:1–5. In Joshua 11:1–5 in particular, what is described is a powerful array of troops and weaponry waiting to attack Israel. But in both Joshua 10 and Joshua 11 Israel successfully defeats the aggressive threat with the destruction of these armies and major cities, again interpreted using the idea of *herem*. What these accounts describe then is another form of response to Yahweh, as seen in terms of the reaction of various hostile kings towards Israel – outsiders are confirmed as outsiders here. Here, in these most developed 'battle accounts' in Joshua, the conquest proceeds as a defensive reaction against military aggression.[13]

Whilst the story dwells on the warfare in Joshua 10:1–28, in Joshua 10:29–11:23 we have only brief, stylized reports of conquest. We saw in the last chapter that comparison with other ancient Near Eastern texts revealed that motifs such as stones falling from heaven and the inducing of fear and panic in the enemy were standard features used in the telling of stories like this and so it would seem likely that we are not intended to take reports such as these, and of the sun and moon standing still in 10:12–14, as literal historical reports that tell us how God can 'suspend the laws of nature'. To be concerned with such questions would seem to be to miss the point of the story. Rather, what we have is an exciting and gripping way of telling a good story, a story told using standard motifs. Moreover, there are clues to the properly mythical nature of Joshua in the conclusion of the conquest here. The report of conquest closes with a report of the annihilation of the Anakim (or Anakites) (11:21–22). But the Anakim are not just a normal group of people. Together with the descendants of Amalek, the Rephaim, and the Nephilim, these groups represent 'mythical' groups of primordial scary beings that share some human characteristics. They are, however, associated with a historical people group, the Amorites. Indeed, from what we know of the 'mythical existence' of these shadowy creatures from other ancient Near Eastern texts, especially Ugaritic texts, we can see that the Old Testament tends to draw the identities of these groups together more generally, conflating and almost (deliberately?) confusing them.[14] Num 13:33 reports that the Anakim are descendents of the Nephilim, who are giants. The Anakim are also said to be giants (Num. 13:28 and Deut. 9:2). But Deuteronomy 2:10–11 reports that the Anakim are considered as Rephaim, and Joshua reports that all the Anakim in the land of Israel were destroyed. But whilst Deuteronomy 3:11 suggests that Og was the last of the Rephaim, Joshua 12:4 and 13:12 have Og as *one of the last* of the Rephaim. Either way, these notes restrict the existence of these figures to a prototypical past. Deuteronomy 4:47 and 31:4 has Og as an Amorite (cf. Josh. 2:10, etc), and so the Amorites are associated with the Rephaim. Amos 2:9–10 has Amorites as giants, and Joshua 10:10 has Sihon and Og as Amorite kings east of the Jordan, in addition to Amorite kings west of the Jordan (Josh. 2:10; 5:1; 9:1, 10; 10:5, 6, 12; 11:3 and 12:2). However, the Amalekites are not found in Joshua, and only occur in Deuteronomy in 25:17 and 19, occurring mainly in Judges and Samuel. The effect of this rather bewildering and disorientating set of associations is to confuse and blur the differences between these various 'pre-historical' groups to paint a picture of non-human, stereotypical, large, scary, baddies that are portrayed as the ancestors of groups hostile to Israel.

So by reporting in the conclusion of Joshua 11:21–22 that the conquest came to completion with the extermination of the Anakim and their towns, Joshua 11 takes on an apologetic character in that the conquest results in the elimination of shadowy, giant pre-historic warrior kings – an elimination of creatures embodying evil perhaps. Setting these shadowy figures of the past, as seen in the Ugaritic materials, in this 'historical narrative' highlights the 'mythological' nature of Joshua, showing it to be set in a prototypical distant past.

But it is interesting that Joshua 11 has this apologetic character, something that is heightened in 11:19–20, for here it seems that the locals might have had the opportunity to make peace, yet their hearts were hardened. This is an interesting note, for there is no indication that this would ever have been a possibility in Deuteronomy. So, returning to the idea that *herem* might function symbolically in the narrative as a 'test', it would seem that in Joshua 10–11 various local kings are reported as acting with hostility towards Israel when 'confronted with *herem*'. This aggressive response then confirms their status as outsiders, as non-Israel, unlike Joshua and the Israelites who, apart from Achan, are portrayed as unswervingly obedient in response to the *herem* command. The status of the aggressive locals as outsiders is confirmed through their death, whilst the status of the Israelites is confirmed with their entry into rest through the fulfilment of God's promises (11:23).

### Joshua 12: list of defeated kings

Joshua 12 concludes the first half of Joshua with a list of defeated kings, a list that serves to make Joshua look rather like a 'conquest account', although as we have seen, it is far from a conquest account with there being rather little space given to the details of warfare. Instead, much space is given to the Jordan crossing, to the ritual procession around Jericho, and to the stories of Rahab, Achan, and the Gibeonites.

### Summary of Joshua 1–12 and its relationship to Joshua 13–22

So, to summarize the first half of Joshua, we see that we have a series of symbolic stories that centre around the issue of how people respond to Yahweh as symbolized in response to *herem*, and how such response relates to whether people are reckoned to be truly 'within Israel', a theme that unifies the first half of Joshua. Although the story is set in the context of conquest, it is not really about conquest. Conquest is the backdrop for stories that make one think carefully about the construction of the identity of the community of those who worship Yahweh. Joshua 1 – 12 is about establishing the true identity of Israel, and what this is defined by and against. It is defined by those who confess Yahweh, are obedient, and exemplify characteristics such as *hesed* (steadfast love). It is defined against those who are disobedient, who steal and covet, and who show aggression towards Israel. Joshua thus raises the question of what attitude the community of Israel ought to have towards itself and towards others. When are ethnic Israelites to be shunned? When are 'surprising non-Israelites' to be welcomed?

It is in this sense that Joshua finds its enactment, and this is where the 'ethics of Joshua' are located – how Joshua is 'acted out' in daily life. It is *not about genocide*. Returning to Victor Turner's comments on myth introduced in chapter 2, we see that *at the literal level the narrative is amoral or even immoral. But this is a common trait of myths, and it is often not where their significance lies*. In other words, *myths do not provide description of or models for behaviour, at least not at the literal or descriptive level of the text taken at face value*.

This is important when we come to rather troubling statements such as we find in Joshua 10:40, 'So Joshua defeated the whole land, the hill country and the Negeb and the lowland and the slopes, and all their kings; he left no one remaining, but utterly destroyed [*herem*] all that breathed, as the LORD God of Israel commanded.' Whilst reports such as this have been taken as expressing the 'theology of Joshua' and thus saying rather disturbing things about God (or at least how Israel perceived God), we have seen that there are other things going on in the story of Joshua. *Herem* has more 'literary' and 'symbolic' functions; functions that are understood well using the tools of neo-structuralism introduced in chapter 2. For example, we noted earlier how reports such as 10:40 serve to bolster the character of Joshua, helping us to interpret the more ambiguous parts of the book – since Joshua is portrayed as being completely obedient, his involvement in sparing Rahab and the Gibeonites tends to imply that it was right that they were spared. Hence when 10:40 is read in conjunction with the rest of the book, where people like Rahab are spared, and in the theological context of the Bible as a whole, it seems that reports like this should be understood precisely in the kind of way that Turner suggests. These are not literal descriptive reports that are designed to tell us about the nature of God or of Israel's early existence.

Indeed, we see that Joshua's significance is discovered through more 'structural level' concerns, relating to questions of categorizing and defining insiders and outsiders and their relationships. Joshua is concerned with the question of how the community defines its identity in terms of response to God (symbolized in *herem*), and how this form of definition is given content. For example, the insider is defined as one who acts with *hesed* (steadfast love), and the outsider defined as one who covets. But Joshua reflects an important ideological transformation of the book of Deuteronomy, and this it seems is what Joshua is largely concerned with, even though it reinforces much that is central to Deuteronomy, such as obedience to the law. In this way we can see that it is Joshua 5:13–15 rather than 10:40 that may in fact be central to a 'theology of Joshua', for in 5:13–15 the commander of Yahweh's army's response to Joshua refuses precisely the sort of categorization of 'us' and 'them' that the stories in Joshua likewise challenge. Yahweh is not simply to be viewed as one who can be co-opted on to an ethnically defined Israel's side. Rather, the issue that 5:13–15 raises is that of appropriate response to Yahweh.

Apart from a reference back to Joshua 7 in Joshua 22 there are, perhaps surprisingly, no more references to *herem* in Joshua. This reflects the different purposes of the two main sections of Joshua, and their different origins too, as we saw in chapter 3. Whilst Joshua 1 –12 is concerned with a narrative portraying the entrance to the land in a deuteronomistic setting, Joshua 13–22 portrays the settlement of the land in a priestly setting. But as we have just seen, Joshua 1–12 is not just, or even essentially, about describing the entrance to the land. Rather, it is a more 'prophetic' kind of story that imaginatively uses the setting of entrance to the land to make Israel consider just what it is that properly makes up her response to Yahweh as expressed in relationships with and attitudes to others. In the same way, we shall see that Joshua 13–22 is not just concerned with the settlement of the land – there is more going on here. Indeed, we shall discover that these two narratives, the deuteronomistic narrative set in the context of conquest and the priestly narrative set in the context of settlement reflect two narratives from different traditions that provide two *different but complementary portraits* of the nature of Israelite identity in response to Yahweh. The combination, or redaction of these two stories along with Joshua 23–24 into the book that we now have provides a mature reflection on the nature of Israelite responsiveness to Yahweh.

However, one important difference between the deuteronomistic (Josh. 1–12) and priestly (Josh. 13–22) sections of Joshua is the portrayal of the conquest as complete or incomplete. It has been one of the often-noted historical difficulties of Joshua that there are different reports of the completeness of the conquest. Some parts report a *complete* conquest (e.g. 11:16 and 23) whilst others report a *partial* conquest (15:63, 16:10 and 17:13). But this is precisely the sort of 'stumbling block' that Origen referred to (see chapter 1) that suggests that the significance of a narrative such as Joshua is not to be found in its 'historical sense'. Indeed, the portrayal of the degree of the completeness of the conquest serves different rhetorical functions in the two parts of the book. In the deuteronomistic section (Josh. 1–12) the completeness of the conquest is tied up with questions of obedience and of approving the treatment of Rahab, Achan, the Gibeonites and the various hostile kings. By portraying the conquest as complete the story evokes complete obedience and thus the 'correctness' of the way that Rahab, Achan and the Gibeonites were dealt with. Remember that Joshua is subtlety challenging and qualifying the 'dogmatism' of Deuteronomy 7:1–5, and so this needs to be done carefully if it is to win acceptance, as is the case with any controversial change in ideology. The completeness of the conquest affirms the obedience of Joshua and the Israelites, as well as reflecting the fulfilment of the promise of the land as expressed in Joshua 21:43–45, a deuteronomistic addition to the otherwise priestly Joshua 13–22. But note here also that this completeness of conquest is tied to the idea of rest (21:44, cf. 11:23) indicating that for Israel the 'goal' of Joshua is not warfare but rest and peace. On the other hand, the incompleteness of the conquest in Joshua 13–22 indicates that there is still work for Israel to do in the settlement of the land and life in it – it is an ongoing task to settle the land. Joshua is not a report of a distant past to be studied as an interesting history book, but rather a book that is a resource for living each day. Every day Israel had to consider how it related to 'others' living in the land, and how to settle in the land and possess it. By portraying the conquest as incomplete in Joshua 13–22 it allows for the text to have a direct relevance to the ongoing daily life of Israel.

## Joshua 13–22: the land

Joshua 13–22 narrates the settlement of Israel in the land, describing the areas that each tribe is to inherit and possess. At one level Joshua 13–22 is important for Israel because it establishes geographical boundaries, and thus it is important in a political sense for the construction of Israel's identity. But it is worth noting the nature of the material here. The geographical boundary descriptions here do not agree that closely with other descriptions of Israel's boundaries given in the Old Testament. Indeed, the boundary descriptions introduced in Joshua 13:1–7 do not even agree with what follows in Joshua, although the boundaries in Joshua 13:1–7 do reflect the boundary descriptions in Numbers 34. But these geographical boundaries differ again from those in Ezekiel 47–48. Moreover, from what we know of historical matters the boundary lists in Joshua 13–22 seem to have been subject to continual revision with the text that we now have representing a continually amended list.[15] In other words, this is another pointer to the nature of the material that we have in Joshua – it is a 'living' text that both shaped and was shaped by the community of Israel as she encountered new circumstances and challenges in her existence.

However, Joshua 13–22 is about more than boundary lists. Joshua 20 establishes cities of refuge and Joshua 21 levitcial cities throughout the land. These were important institutions in the makeup of Israel, so, as in Joshua 5, we see here the establishment of institutions that will reflect the pattern of life that Israel is to live in the land, and what is important to her as a society. But more than this, note how in Joshua 13–22 reports of boundary lists are woven around stories of particular people. And these stories are important. Rather like the stories

of Rahab, Achan and the Gibeonites in Joshua 1–12, these stories map out something of what it means to live as a faithful
Israelite in response to Yahweh. Inherent in these characters is
displayed (positively and negatively) something of what it is
that is to characterize the Israelite.

Caleb (Josh. 14:6–15) is an example of one who follows
Yahweh 'wholeheartedly' (Josh. 14:8, 9 and 14). It is a rare characteristic (it only occurs elsewhere in Num. 14:24; 32:11, 12;
Deut. 1:36 and 1 Kgs. 11:6), and exemplifies genuine responsiveness to Yahweh.[16] Here it interprets and is interpreted by
Caleb's actions. Caleb drives out the Anakim (14:12), those
mysterious, mythical, scary 'people', and receives a blessing
from Joshua (14:13). However, he is a Kenizzite (14:6), and thus
not a truly pedigreed Israelite, perhaps emphasized in the
genealogical note in 14:14.[17] So Caleb is of questionable pedigree, yet acts in an exemplary way, not unlike Rahab. Caleb is
portrayed as one who takes bold initiatives based upon trusting in Yahweh being with him as a result of Yahweh's promise,
showing what it is that is to characterize the faithful Israelite.
Caleb's story concludes with the note that the land had rest
from war (14:15), which has the effect of adding to this positive
appraisal of Caleb and his actions.

Together with the other stories in Joshua 13–19, Caleb's
story indicates that bold initiative-taking like this in response
to a promise of Yahweh is what is required of Israel for her to
possess the land successfully, such as is the case with the
Danites (19:47–48). They attack and settle a town outside their
inheritance because they had trouble in possessing their allot-
ted territory, showing bold initiative. And Caleb says in
15:16–19 that boldness and strength is required to win his
daughter, Achsah, in marriage by capturing Kiriath Sepher,
which Othniel does. Following this Achsah herself makes a
bold request of her father, which he grants.[18] Similarly,
Zelophehad's request for an inheritance for his daughters
(17:3–4) reflects a certain 'boldness', but is associated with the
promise in Numbers (Num. 36), and his daughters duly
receive an inheritance. Whilst inheritance by daughters is
reported elsewhere in the ancient Near East,[19] the report of
such inheritance here, and the report of Achsah's initiative,

along with Rahab's story, might imply that the Old Testament is rather less 'irredeemably patriarchal' than some might suggest. In particular, these stories indicate that patriarchy is rather less essential to Israelite identity than might be assumed. Or, just as Joshua 1–12 seeks to qualify the dogmatism of Deuteronomy 7:1–5, perhaps here Joshua is seeking to cause the rethink of patriarchal attitudes.

However, on a negative note, when the people of Joseph complain about their lack of land (17:14), Joshua's response is to suggest that they boldly take more land. But they complain that the land is associated with Rephaim (those scary bad guys again), and with Canaanites with iron chariots. Their complaint contrasts with Caleb. Caleb went up against the Anakim and large cities, whereas the Josephites are afraid to fight the Rephaim and iron chariots. They lack the required boldness and courage, and their story ends on a rather ambiguous note. Joshua reassures them that they can take the land – but will they?

Thus we see that Joshua 13–19 explores questions of what it is that is to characterize the nature of Israel's response to Yahweh so as to settle in the land and find rest. Like Joshua 1–12 it contains some surprises – people of questionable ethnic pedigree (Caleb) can respond more faithfully than some 'ethnic insiders'. Moreover, women can exemplify faithful responsiveness to Yahweh in ways that exceed some of their male counterparts. What is required to settle the land and live in rest and peace in the land is bold initiative-taking based on the promises and commands of Yahweh.

But what is interesting here is that in this priestly account of the settlement of the land there is a possible allusion to the priestly creation narrative in Genesis 1. The allusion is supplied by the relatively rare term *kabash*, meaning something like 'subdue', which occurs in Gen 1:28 ('God blessed them, and God said to them, "Be fruitful and multiply, and fill the earth and subdue [*kabash*] it; and have dominion over the fish of the sea and over the birds of the air and over every living thing that moves upon the earth."') and Joshua 18:1 ('Then the whole congregation of the Israelites assembled at Shiloh, and set up the tent of meeting there. The land lay subdued [*kabash*] before them.'). The use of the term in Genesis 1:28 has come to be seen as increasingly problematic as our ecological awareness has been raised, with Genesis 1:28 being sometimes taken (or being assumed to be taken) as a mandate for the exploitation of the environment. But in a sense perhaps Josh 18:1 indicates what it means to fulfil this command, at least for ancient Israel. What Joshua indicates then is that the mandate in Genesis 1:28 finds (at least partial) fulfilment when Israel is living in the land and living in covenantal relationship with Yahweh, as made concrete through a life lived as guided by the Law of Moses.[20] But remember that the land also has a symbolic sense – life in the land symbolizes the blessings of a life lived in relationship with Yahweh, symbolizing the covenant. So in a sense then the land – or perhaps even life – is 'subdued' when a group of people, Israel, is established who are living in proper relationship with Yahweh. So again we see how reading the narrative from its proper perspective as discourse – here, a priestly perspective – indicates what it means to read the narrative in a fitting way, highlighting the concerns of the story. Here, we see how the concern with settlement in the land is part of a bigger concern – the fulfilment of the creation mandate, and it helps to illustrate just what this mandate means. The creation mandate is not about exploiting the environment. Instead, it is about 'settling' into a life of covenant relationship with Yahweh, the blessings of which are expressed by dwelling securely in a land of abundance.

But the issue of the land – both in general ecological terms and in the specific terms of the land of Israel – is a difficult one, especially in our own contemporary global context where tensions run high. Does Joshua have more to say on the issue of the land? It is in Joshua 22 that we find Israel's identity in terms of the land tackled. The land is something that is of key importance in the priestly tradition – Yahweh dwells in the land of Israel, land that must be 'pure' in order for him to dwell there in the tabernacle or temple. Indeed, it is this sort of theology that is partly behind the nature of the crisis of the exile (Has God abandoned Israel?). But Joshua 22 raises the very question of the nature of the land and its relationship to Israel's identity from within this kind of priestly perspective.

Joshua 22 will suggest what is perhaps a challenging conclusion for the priestly tradition, much as Joshua 6–11 is rather
challenging for some aspects of the deuteronomistic tradition.

Joshua 22 tells of the building of an altar by the transjordanians (that is, those living on the 'wrong' side of the Jordan
(the eastern side), outside the Promised Land) near the Jordan.
The cisjordanians (those living on the 'correct' side of the
Jordan, i.e. those living west of the Jordan in the Promised
Land) object to the construction of this altar, resulting in a dialogue which reaches an amicable resolution in the end where
the cisjordanians eventually accept the altar as legitimate.[21] But
the construction of the altar and the following dialogue is
designed to raise a number of issues relating to the land, unity,
and worship, and it is these concerns that drive the story. The
altar is described as a big and imposing altar (22:10) – there is
no mistaking it! However, its location relative to the Jordan is
ambiguous, with the Hebrew being deliberately obscure
(22:10–11). Which side of the Jordan is it on? The altar's construction, location and use raises three main concerns. First,
there is the question of the transjordanian land, and whether it
is 'unclean' (*tama*, 22:19). Secondly, the question of where legitimate offerings may be made (22:19, 23, 26 and 28–29), something associated with the question of the purpose of the
altar. Thirdly, the story is concerned with the unity of Israel,
especially in future generations. Are the transjordanians part
of the people Israel (22:24–28, 34), despite living 'across the
Jordan', i.e., outside the land of Israel?

The question of the 'uncleanness' of the land raised in
22:19 by the cisjordanians is not developed or resolved
explicitly in the story. However, as the dispute is resolved in
favour of the transjordanians, the question is resolved implicitly. Either the land is not 'unclean', or the purity of the land
is shown not to be a crucial issue. But in 22:9 it is clear that
Yahweh has given the transjordanians the land 'on the wrong
side' of the Jordan as an inheritance, and so the cisjordanian
question reflects a tendency of the community to *construct
boundaries that go beyond those set by Yahweh*. Indeed, we have
seen that much of Joshua is concerned with boundaries in
different ways. Here we have a geographical boundary that

in some sense reflects boundaries within the community of the people Israel.

Attention is also drawn here to the nature and significance of the Jordan as a boundary, or not, as the case may be, through the use of the verb *avar* again (recall the significance of *avar* in the Jordan crossing in Joshua 3–4 discussed above), or rather the *lack of use* of *avar* here, apart from in 22:19. We saw earlier that *avar* symbolized 'crossing' into or out of the community of Israel. And indeed in 22:19 the word *avar* is used by the cisjordanians to indicate that they believe that the transjordanians must 'cross' back into Israel, both in the sense of geography and community. In the eyes of the cisjordanians the transjordanians have crossed out of the community of true Israel – they must cross back in, symbolized in the crossing of the Jordan. But the narrator carefully avoids the use of *avar* in his telling of the story and in his interpretation to indicate that the transjordanians have not in fact crossed out of the community of Israel.

A significant part of the dialogue here concerns the function of the altar. The transjordanians stress their intention in constructing the altar in terms of remembrance and unity. It is not for offerings and sacrifices, i.e. it is not a rival altar upon which illegitimate offerings might be made, and so divide the community of Israel. The altar is to serve a unifying function rather than a divisive one. The cisjordanians appeal to Achan's story (Josh. 7) and the sin at Peor (Num. 25) to express their concern. They understand the construction of the altar as an act of rebellion like the actions described in these stories, action that will bring the wrath of Yahweh on all Israel. This concern is considered by Phinehas, who is appointed by the cisjordanians to investigate the building of the altar. Upon hearing the transjordanian perspective, Phinehas is satisfied with what they have done. The altar is not for offerings, and its construction does not mark an act of rebellion. It is not an attempt to divide Israel, but rather to unify Israel. In fact Phinehas ironically inverts the cisjordanian interpretation of the altar and the fears that they have. It is actually the cisjordanians that have risked divine wrath, and the transjordanians who avert it (22:31). So whilst the cisjordanians saw a reflection of Achan in the

transjordanian action, it is actually the cisjordanians themselves who reflect Achan and risk divine wrath, demonstrating
another ironic reversal of what is *apparently* the case! Having
Phinehas as the one who judges the case here grants the ver-
dict authority, for this is the same Phinehas who acted zeal-
ously to halt the plague against the Israelites at Peor, the inci-
dent referred to by the cisjordanians (see Num. 25:6–13). In a
sense then Joshua 22 is similar to the stories of Rahab and
Achan. Despite appearances, and the traditional position,
Rahab reflects the true Israelite, unlike Achan. Despite appearances, it is the cisjordanian action that threatens God's wrath,
not the transjordanian action. And whilst Rahab and Achan's
stories show that issues of ethnicity are not finally determinative for Israelite identity, so Joshua 22 shows that geography
and land are not finally determinative either.

To look at this in terms of symbol, perhaps the problem with
the perspective reflected in Deuteronomy 7:1–5 is that it takes
ethnicity (rather than what it symbolizes) as the 'absolute', and
perhaps the problem with the cisjordanian perspective is that
it takes land and geography (rather than what they symbolize)
as the 'absolute'. In other words, ethnic identity symbolizes
the presence of a historically 'called' group of people, a group
called as a family originally to be in covenantal relationship
with Yahweh. The land symbolizes that covenant and relationship. Together with the rest of Joshua, Joshua 22 indicates that
many of the expected ways of 'defining Israel' are qualified
even if not rejected, and it is interesting that this concern of
clarifying the nature of the symbol is reflected in both the
deuteronomistic and priestly sections of Joshua, both urging
caution against confusing the symbol with the reality. The
cisjordanians had assumed that the symbol and the reality
were identical.

## Joshua 23–24: Israel's ongoing response

The two main sections of Joshua are now complete. These are
drawn together in the closing exhortations of Joshua 23–24.
The speeches in these two closing chapters seem to reflect two

complementary perspectives regarding what Israel's ongoing response to Yahweh ought to look like in the light of the rest of the book. These chapters bring the dim and distant yet formative prototypical past of Israel into the present. Joshua 23 is deuteronomistic in flavour, looking back to Deuteronomy 7:1–5 in particular, whilst Joshua 24 represents a more general reflection on the storyline of the Pentateuch, although one that it is, as we shall see, spectacularly selective (there is no mention of the giving of the law at Sinai) so as to call forth a particular kind of response.

What is interesting in Joshua 23 is that *Israel is to take an entirely passive role in the possession of the land from now on*. The 'driving out' of the locals is to be left entirely in Yahweh's hands (23:5). There is no reference to *herem* here. Israel's role is described entirely in terms of obeying the law and of avoiding intermarriage, covenants with the locals and the worship of their gods (23:6–7) in language reminiscent of Deuteronomy 7:1–5. Israel's role is to 'hold fast' to Yahweh (23:8). The remainder of Joshua 23 is a warning against turning away from Yahweh. Whilst all Yahweh's promises have been fulfilled in bringing Israel into the land, if Israel turns away from Yahweh Israel will perish from the land (23:16). Indeed, notice the language here – Israel will be driven from the land if she transgresses (*avar*, the same word for crossing in Josh. 3–4) the covenant (23:16). Again, the idea of 'crossing' is associated with life in the land and with the covenant as we have seen – the land symbolizes the covenant and vice versa. Moreover, it is interesting that it is only now when we reach Joshua 23 that the problem of idolatry and the worship of other gods is raised. One might well have expected it to come up sooner in Joshua, perhaps as an apologetic to justify the conquest. If the locals were all portrayed as immoral idolaters then it would ease the justification of their genocide perhaps. But we do not find this in Joshua, suggesting that Joshua is not concerned with justifying conquest, as we have seen, and that the book is about something different. It is also interesting that there is no reference to *herem* here in Joshua 23, and neither is there any call to Israel to fulfil Deuteronomy 7:1–5 by practicing violence here. In a sense then Joshua 23 provides a 'commentary' or 'homily' on Joshua to indicate the kind of way in which the reader is to respond. Joshua 1–22 reflects a mythical and highly symbolic past world, whereas Joshua 23 seeks to connect this mythical and imaginative world of the past with the actual everyday world of the reader in the present. The charge to Israel is to practice separation *from* the locals *to* Yahweh, made concrete in the observance of the law on the one hand, and, specifically, by the avoidance of intermarriage and covenants with the locals on the other, as per Deuteronomy 7:1–5 – but, as we have seen, not quite as per Deuteronomy 7:1–5. In other words, Joshua 23 encourages the enactment of Deuteronomy 7:1–5, but Deuteronomy 7:1–5 *as read through the rest of Joshua*. Joshua envisages separations like Deuteronomy 7:1–5, but of a rather different nature. Joshua envisages separations based on responsiveness to Yahweh, rather than with rigid regard to genealogy or geography.

The farewell speech of Joshua 24 shares a number of similarities with Joshua 23. But it calls for a different kind of response from that in Joshua 23. It calls for a response of 'choosing Yahweh', and encourages the reader to ponder the demanding nature of this choice. By commencing the speech in 24:2–13 with the story of Abraham as a worshipper of other gods, but as one whom Yahweh led out from the land beyond the river, and concluding the speech with Israel's safe possession of the promised land, all at Yahweh's initiative, it shows that Israel owes her existence entirely to Yahweh and thus of her need for him. But, rhetorically speaking, precisely because of this 'grace', the possibility of a reversal is implied. Yahweh can just as easily cast Israel back across the river, outside the land, outside relationship with him. Choosing Yahweh and serving him (24:14ff) is the response that is sought, a response that will lead to continued enjoyment of and blessing in the land. On the other hand, choosing to worship idols and other gods will lead to an 'undoing', a return to the place where Abraham started from.

Again, we see the importance of crossing (*avar*) here and how it draws together the inter-related ideas of land and life with Yahweh as they symbolize each other. Joshua here suggests that what makes people outsiders is serving other gods.

This rhetoric and the response that it calls for may explain why there is no interest in the law, or indeed in any covenant (such as the covenant with Abraham) in 24:2–13. For what is important and developed here is Yahweh's unilateral action on behalf of Israel, with the implication that he can simply 'undo' all this history and return Israel to a pre-Abrahamic existence. If the idea of the following of a law were introduced it might imply the earning of a status for Israel – that she earns and deserves her life as a nation in the land. So what we probably have in this selective account is powerful rhetoric that will go on to call for Israel's response. The speech in Joshua 24 encourages the reader to see that here and now is the time where response and mutual commitment is called for.

But what then about Joshua's rather shocking response to Israel's positive response to the call to choose for Yahweh? The purpose of this surprising response would seem to be explained in terms of rhetoric once again. Joshua wants Israel to grasp and to ponder the demanding nature of the choice presented and all that it entails. It is not to be made lightly, and it is not a choice without difficulties. Through this 'delaying' of the acceptance of Israel's response the reader is moved into a fuller and more serious realization of the character of Yahweh and of the nature of the choice that is to be made for him, even if it is the only choice that makes sense as indicated in the previous few verses. 'True Israel' is made up of those who gladly choose to worship and serve Yahweh, a choice expressed in living by *torah* (the Mosaic Law) and avoiding competing, idolatrous allegiances expressed in a life of boldness on the one hand and *hesed* (steadfast love and faithfulness) on the other.

## Summary

So let us now summarize what the book of Joshua seems to be about. The book as we now have it reads as if it described the fulfilment of Deuteronomy 7. But as we have seen, it is not written to be a straightforward report of how Deuteronomy 7 was actually fulfilled. Whilst Joshua is a story set in the prototypical context of conquest, it is not really a story about conquest or genocide. It does not relish in reports of violence or battle. There are indicators such as the nature of the spy mission, the location of Rahab's house in the wall that falls, and the different portraits of complete and partial conquest that, within the world of the text alone, point away from understanding the story as being concerned with a straight-forward historical description of events. Moreover, the amount of space given in the text to the crossing of the Jordan, the rit-ual procession around Jericho, the stories of Rahab, Achan, the Gibeonites and the transjordanians, and the lack of 'military' details in these stories points away from understanding Joshua to be really concerned with genocide, warfare or violence.

We saw in chapter 3 that *herem* was not significant in the Old Testament as a description of a historical practice of warfare or conquest. Rather, we saw that in Deuteronomy, and Deuter-onomy 7 in particular, what the author of the text was doing with the concept of *herem* was to use it symbolically to com-mand the separation of Israel from non-Israel. And we saw this idea reflected in texts like Ezra 9:1–2.[22] *Herem* in Deuteron-omy 7 thus has a literary and ideological function rather than an essentially descriptive function. Likewise in Joshua we have seen that *herem* also serves a symbolic, literary function – but one that differs from its function in Deuteronomy even if it is based upon it. In Joshua *herem* appears to symbolize what one might describe as 'divine action in the world', response to which symbolizes response to Yahweh, serving the function of a test that indicates where one's heart and true identity are located. When one is confronted with *herem* (in the world of the text) does one show oneself to be 'for Yahweh' or 'against Yahweh'? In other words, this precisely reflects the inversion of Joshua's question to the commander of the Lord's army in 5:13–15. It is not important to ask whether God is 'on our side' but rather what is important is to ask if we are 'on God's side', to put it rather crudely. What Joshua 1–12 provides us with then is a matrix of test cases that probe the question of the rela-tionship between apparent and real identity in terms of response to Yahweh as symbolized in response to *herem*. Of course, *herem* literally enacted may well be an immoral idea – but as we have seen, this is not the issue for myth, as in myth such symbols are not urging actions to copy or approve if they were to occur in the 'real world' rather than the 'world of the text'.

We can summarize the responses to *herem* in Joshua in a table:

| Person/<br>group | Initial<br>status | Response to<br>*herem* | Nature of<br>response | 'Revealed'<br>status |
|---|---|---|---|---|
| Rahab<br>(Josh. 2, 6) | Outsider | Glorifies<br>Yahweh and<br>*hesed* | Positive | Insider |
| Achan<br>(Josh. 6–8) | Insider | Coveting, etc. | Negative | Outsider<br>(death) |
| Local kings<br>(Josh. 10–11) | Outsiders | Aggression | Negative | Outsiders<br>(death) |
| Josh.<br>(*passim*) | Insider | Obedience | Positive | Insider |
| Gibeonites<br>(Josh. 9) | Outsiders | No response<br>*per se* | Ambiguous | Ambiguous<br>(slavery) |

**Table 2: The construction of identity as response to *herem* in Joshua**

Having set up these 'test cases' in terms of response to *herem*, what the narrative then implies is a re-think of what it is that makes up the identity of Israel – the community of those who respond faithfully to Yahweh – and how the community is to respond to others. Joshua implies a re-think of the nature of the separation that Deuteronomy 7:1–5 envisages, a separation that is based largely upon an ethnic or genealogical construction of identity. Joshua does not demolish the idea of separation from certain sorts of people, as we see in Joshua 23 which reasserts the need for separation. But the nature of this separation now looks different in the light of the rest of Joshua. So what Joshua actually does then is to challenge the tradition represented in Deuteronomy from the inside, as the inside is often the best place from which to seek change. It uses the very language and concerns of the tradition to try and turn the tradition around. But this is very risky, because the text of Joshua is then open to misunderstanding – to advocating genocide when it is in fact a story set within the context of a story of genocide to try to challenge the tradition using some of its favourite language.

However, Joshua goes beyond questioning identity at this level. For in Joshua 22 we see that the centrality of the land in defining Israel is qualified. What Joshua 22 indicates is that the land symbolizes the relationship of Israel with Yahweh – the land is not the 'reality' itself, even if it shares in this reality in some sense, by being an abundant and fertile land that brings blessings, for example. So in a sense then one could say that Joshua is concerned with the appropriate use of symbolism, and that one must not confuse the symbol with the reality. So in ethnic terms, the response of an ethnic group stemming from a single family is symbolic of response to Yahweh's call, and in geographic terms, life in the land symbolizes life in covenantal relationship with Yahweh.

Finally, Joshua 13–21 reflects something of the establishment of tribal inheritances. But this section is also concerned with displaying the sort of characteristics that will exemplify the Israelites who are successful in inheriting and dwelling in the land. This section complements the rest of the book, although we see that it functions in a slightly different way.

But, to return to the anthropological analysis of myth and symbol, it is interesting that one characteristic of the transmission and use of myth and symbol is that they tend to become 'tired' or 'historicized' as we saw in chapter 2. That is, myths and symbols, which originally have a concrete first-order sense and a more abstract and perhaps existential second-order sense find their significance 'collapsed' into the literal sense, with the second-order sense being lost. The true significance of the symbol is lost, with the literal sense of the symbol becoming all that can be perceived. And this is precisely what has happened with the book of Joshua – its symbolic significance has been lost, with the book being read instead in terms of a description of a history of genocide.

So, Joshua is about re-thinking what constitutes the nature of Israel's identity, and what the 'reality' of this identity is. The anthropological approaches to myth that we discussed in chapter 2 have helped to illuminate that this is what is going on. Victor Turner's work helped us to see that myths are not models to follow in a straightforward sense, even as they call for 'enactment' in daily life. Seth Kunin's development of structuralism allowed us to see the kind of things that Joshua is concerned with, and helps to show how to give content to the 'enactment' of the myth in terms of what response to God ought to look like.

# 5.

# Reading Joshua as Christian Scripture

### Reading old texts in new contexts: Joshua in the canon

In chapter 4 we sought to understand what the book of Joshua was about as discourse. We asked, 'What are the concerns of this text and what was it composed to achieve in the kinds of context in which it would have been heard and used 'originally'?' But this is not the same as reading Joshua *as Christian Scripture* today, and I suggest that it is within the canonical as well as the contemporary context that Joshua ought to be read by the Christian if it is to be read well today. In very general terms, we saw in chapter 2 that anthropological work on myth coupled with Paul Ricoeur's work on the nature and use of literary texts indicates that the significance of texts such as Joshua is not something that is static, timeless, and the same for everyone everywhere. Rather, the significance of texts like Joshua is *dynamic* and *ever developing*. This is because myths, or important texts, are read alongside new important texts, myths, philosophies, ideologies or events that bring new concerns to the older texts. So for example how does the coming of Christ, and the subsequent reflection on his life, death and resurrection in the New Testament, affect the way in which we read Joshua? How do we understand *herem*, even in its symbolic sense as relating to separation, in the light of Christ?

Indeed, if we think about it this changing significance is obvious for some biblical texts – the significance of the book of

Leviticus is very different for Christians today than it was for ancient Israelites. So an Old Testament text can be cherished and appropriately read in very different ways in different contexts. Thus the original significance of a text does not carry straight across to its significance in a new context because fresh questions are put to the text, especially in a Christian context where an Old Testament text is read through the lens of further discernment and revelation. Or, in the language of myth, older myths are read in the light of new myths which affect the way in which the older myths are understood – they are transformed, as has been observed in structuralist accounts of myth. New myths and new events affect the way in which older myths find contemporary relevance. But to put the issue this way is simply to re-express (although with some modification) in more general anthropological terms the traditional Christian approach to the Old Testament of typological, allegorical or spiritual reading. When texts of the Old Testament are placed alongside the New Testament, and read in terms of Christ, they take on new significance that is discovered with reference to Christ. This is demonstrated, for instance, in the way that the author of the book of Hebrews develops themes from Leviticus *in the light of Christ*.

But perhaps it will be helpful to consider a non-biblical example to see how this works more generally. To consider an influential text that is foundational for the life of a society in a different context, take the American Declaration of Independence, written in 1776. It contains a clause that 'all men are created equal . . . endowed by their Creator with certain unalienable Rights'. This statement has been foundational for American life and for various rights movements, especially in the twentieth century. This clause was quoted by Martin Luther King Jr. in his 'I Have a Dream' speech. Clearly it has been very influential. But in its original context in the eighteenth century 'men' would have referred to white property-owning males. Today it is taken as a statement indicating the equality of *all* people. In other words, what we understand the text as saying to us – how it addresses us in our context – is different, *although continuous with* what the text sought to achieve originally. The significance of the text is different in our context from that of its original context.[1] Alternatively, to take a recent non-biblical example from the British legal sphere, I am writing this chapter shortly after the British government is seeking to use 'anti-terror' laws to freeze the assets of Icelandic banks and companies in the wake of the global 'credit crunch', a move that has resulted in the Icelandic government attempting to sue the British government in the European Court of Human Rights.[2] Whilst the use of the American Declaration of Independence in the way indicated above is generally uncontroversial, the use of 'anti-terror' laws for economic ends is more controversial, probably because such use does not seem to be 'fitting', unlike the development of the Declaration of Independence. These two non-biblical examples indicate that when texts that are in some sense 'authoritative' are read and used in new situations and contexts decisions need to be made regarding the question of what it means to interpret and to use a particular text *well*. The use of texts is as much a question of discernment in the context of the interpreter as it is a question of knowledge about the text as originally produced. Good use of texts arises out of the fruitful 'conversation' between the 'plenitude' (the many possible) and 'fittingness' (the appropriateness) of interpretations of the text. Although the examples I have chosen are from the more legal sphere, the same may be said of more 'literary' or 'poetic' works, works that are steeped in symbolism, symbolism that will evoke different things in different contexts.

The issue then is that of *discerning* what counts as a 'good' use of a text in a new context. And usually we do encounter texts in new contexts, as we are usually at some distance from the author and their context. Here Ricoeur is helpful: he can be understood to imply that there are a 'plenitude' of interpretations of a literary text that indicate different ways in which the text *might* be understood and used as different readers encounter it, but also that for a text to be read and used *well* an interpretation must be 'fitting' to the text as discourse. So, as I suggested above, one might say that the contemporary use of the American Declaration of Independence as outlined above is a fitting exploration of its plenitude that is in continuity with what the text sought to achieve as discourse, whilst the use of anti-terror laws for economic purposes is not, introducing something that is alien. In other words, in this latter case a 'new text' is effectively introduced rather than a proper use of an existing text. Discernment here is crucial, and what counts as fitting can be contested.

The canon of Scripture offers us guidance in terms of exploring the plenitude and fittingness of the interpretation of any particular biblical text. The canon, and the subsequent tradition of its reception and use, shows us the most important ways in which the plenitude of a text like Joshua is to be explored, and explored well, in a Christian context. In a sense the canon (as a composition and discourse itself) both 'opens up' and 'closes down' possibilities for what it means to read a given biblical text well as Christians. So, for example, what about exploring Joshua with regard to being a warrant to commit genocide? This is one way of exploring the text. But it is not, on the whole, fitting with respect to the canon of Scripture. If one assumes that Joshua should be read in the light of the gospels for example, then it is difficult to see how one could seek to legitimate genocide using Joshua when read through the gospels, texts which commend the love of neighbour whoever they may be (the Parable of the Good Samaritan). But, as we have seen, using Joshua as a warrant for genocide is not 'fitting' with respect to what Joshua seems to be trying to achieve originally either. In other words then, for a Christian reader of a biblical text 'fittingness' is a criterion for interpretation that relates both to what the text was originally trying to achieve, and to how it is received and used in the canon of Scripture, and subsequently in the Christian tradition.[3] A good reading of a text like Joshua in a new context (here, a Christian context) respects what the text originally sought to achieve, and respects the exploration and connection of the text with other important texts that are regarded as authoritative and generative for the life of the Christian community.[4] But this is, perhaps, simply a restatement of the approach to reading the Bible that we found in Irenaeus in chapter 1.

What this means for us is that the significance of some features of a text such as Joshua may recede into the background whilst others are developed as the text continues to address new situations in the Christian context. So, for example, much of the book of Leviticus recedes into the background for the Christian when it is read in conjunction with the New Testament (such as the dietary laws), even as certain concerns of the book are developed in new ways, such as one finds with the sacrificial laws in the book of Hebrews. Or, turning to Joshua, in Christian reading of Joshua Rahab's story is developed a good deal in terms of faith,[5] whilst the accounts of the distribution of the land, and of the cities of refuge for example, receive rather little treatment. Indeed, this is reflected in chapter 4, where I said little about these concerns since they recede from view in a Christian reading of the text. So in a way the reading of Joshua presented in chapter 4, whilst not explicitly a Christian reading of Joshua as such, is a reading already influenced by Christian concerns, since in my analysis I allowed certain features of the text to recede into the background.

The issue for us is that of what it means to read Joshua well in a Christian context. This means interpreting the 'world of the text' that it presents, and what it sought to achieve as discourse, through the lens of Scripture as a whole, the Christian tradition, and the concerns of the contemporary reader – such as how Joshua reads in the wake of 9/11. As we have seen, a good contemporary reading should be in continuity with what Joshua sought to 'achieve' (i.e., it should be 'fitting') even if it will not be the same as being a restatement of what Joshua sought to achieve originally (i.e., as its 'plenitude' is explored in the light of new questions). Theologically speaking, this is simply to recognize that God's word is addressed to us as people situated in particular contexts with particular concerns that need to be addressed, calling forth a particular kind of response that will be different in different circumstances. The theology of the biblical texts is that of 'applied theology'. The way that we need to be 'shaped' in our response to God will vary from context to context, even though it is the same God to whom we are responding, with the different ways in which we respond sharing a certain 'family resemblance'. The issues facing ancient Israel were not the same as those facing us. How we respond faithfully will be different from how ancient Israel

responded faithfully simply because we face different challenges and issues. However, the issues are not totally different
or disconnected (issues of money, sex and power are shared by
humanity generally, for example), and so texts like Joshua continue to speak beyond their original context.

But perhaps the biggest challenge that we face is this: How
do we discern the way in which we *ought* to let Joshua continue to speak 'with its own voice'? Perhaps it is too often the case
that when we talk of reading Old Testament texts through the
New Testament we simply impose what we know from the
New Testament onto an Old Testament text. In other words,
where we can find a 'message' in an Old Testament text that
simply agrees with something we find in the New, then we are
happy. But then we are not really reading and using the Old
Testament – we are simply reasserting the New in the dress of
the Old. Alternatively, when we find material, especially
'legal' material, that is *set aside* in the New Testament (such as
the dietary laws of Leviticus, Leviticus 11, compare Acts
10–11), then, on the whole, I think that we are happy to leave
such material in the past as material that no longer has direct
relevance for Christians.[6] But what about Old Testament material that is neither set aside nor clearly developed in the New?
In other words, there is a real problem in terms of discerning
the distinctive voice of the Old Testament and of how this
voice might continue to speak in the shaping of Christian identity. We need to find a way of respecting the 'oldness' of the
Old Testament on the one hand, accepting that it does not
speak to us directly today granted that the material *is* in some
sense 'old' (see Jer. 31:31–34), whilst at the same time recognizing that this Old Testament material witnesses to, and is
revelatory of the same God whom we worship in Christ, and
forms the basis for our understanding of Jesus. It is primarily
through the Old Testament that the New Testament understands and interprets the person and work of Christ.

But this issue – of how we discern continuity or discontinuity – is one reason why I introduced the rather difficult body of
theory of neo-structuralism in chapter 2 since neo-structuralism provides us with a convenient way of identifying and of
speaking about the 'oldness' of the Old Covenant. As we shall

see, it will provide some pointers for discerning whether certain aspects of some Old Testament texts ought to find development or not in the context of the New Covenant.

Remember that we saw that the ancient Israelite worldview 'structure' was characterized by categorizations into mutually exclusive categories that did not permit mediation or transformation, such as is the case with animals that are clean or unclean, Israelites that are priests or non-priests by birth, and people that are either Israelite or non-Israelite. However, in the Christian context we saw that transformation (through conversion) and mediation (through the indwelling of the Holy Spirit) are essential to Christian thinking and identity. This identification of difference between Old and New Testament contexts through neo-structuralism might be a helpful *anthropological* way of studying the *theological* discontinuity between the two covenants. Anthropologically speaking some Old Testament texts may be inherently concerned with *reinforcing* the old structure of ancient Israelite thinking, in which case one would expect such texts to become obsolete in the New Covenant, as we have seen with the animal classifications of Leviticus. But remember that we also saw that in neo-structuralism (as opposed to classical structuralism) myths were understood to be capable of trying to challenge or develop the underlying structure rather than simply reinforcing it. In other words, it might be possible to understand some myths in the Old Testament as trying 'prophetically' to reshape the basic structure of the underlying worldview in a direction that moves towards the Christian one, and one might well say that this is a significant aspect of the revelatory character of such texts since they are generative of a new and perhaps more faithful way of responding to God, anticipating responsiveness to Christ. And indeed it is the myths that are expressive of this 'prophetic reshaping' in the Old Testament that we tend to be familiar with as Christians – the stories of Rahab, Ruth and Naaman (2 Kgs. 5) are well known and used in the Christian context, since these stories have been taken to indicate 'conversion' to God's people. Thus they are, in a rather undeveloped form, expressive of the necessity of conversion that is key to the New Testament, and for this reason the stories continue to be important as imaginative illustrations of such transformation. But other stories in the Old Testament, such as the rape of Dinah and the massacre that follows (Gen. 34), are stories that reinforce the worldview structure that denies transformation and mediation. When such texts are problematic at the narrative level – as myths often are (and as Gen. 34 certainly is) – they do not find use in the Christian context.[7] So neo-structuralism offers a helpful tool to identify Old Testament narrative texts that one might or might not expect to find significance in the Christian context.

Indeed, with Joshua we have, I suggest, a story that in many ways sits very well with the New Covenant at the 'structural level' (in that it is expressive of certain kinds of transformation and mediation), but is more problematic at the 'narrative level', as with many myths, since genocide is part of its subject matter. It is this latter concern that has come to dominate recent Christian reading of Joshua (the narrative level concern), especially in the wake of events such as 9/11. But traditional Christian reading of Joshua tended instinctively (and subconsciously) to focus on the more symbolic structural level concerns of the text (expressed in terms of Rahab's faith, for instance), finding creative ways of dealing with the narrative level concerns, as we shall see below in Origen's reading of Joshua.

But as we saw in chapter 4, since what Joshua sought to 'achieve' is so bound up with structural level concerns (i.e., of insiders and outsiders and their relationships), then it is a good and fitting use of the text to continue to develop these structural concerns over against some of the more problematic elements of the narrative, elements that were *never* the real concern of the text. The narrative here appears to exist largely to serve structural ends relating to the characterization of and relationships between insiders and outsiders. However, one must not dispense with the narrative entirely, for it is through the narrative that *content* is given to structural level concerns. It is through the narrative that the nature of transformation, mediation and faithful response to God – what makes up insiders and outsiders – is expressed. We saw that in Rahab's case content was given to her character as embodying faithful response to God in terms of a risky *hesed* (steadfast love or faithfulness), and the glorification of God. This is readily developed in the Christian context, as we discover in the common use of Rahab's story in early Christian literature. So woven in to Rahab's story is material from which practical application may be deduced. *Hesed* is to characterize the one who responds faithfully to God.

However, reading 'doctrine' off a narrative such as Joshua is not straightforward, as we might expect from Victor Turner's comments on myth in which he notes that myths are often amoral at the level of the narrative, something also identified in neo-structuralist treatment of myth. But this issue – of determining doctrine from an Old Testament narrative – becomes increasingly problematic when the narrative is used in a Christian context because there are two levels of discernment required for the Christian reader. First, the reader must discern what aspects of the narrative are there to give content to actual practice, rather than simply serving literary or structural requirements, in terms of what the myth originally sought to achieve as discourse. Secondly, having made this discernment, the Christian reader must then discern whether or not a given practice deduced from the narrative finds continuity with Christian practice. For example, the confession of sin is of central importance in a Christian context, for confession leads to forgiveness and the restoration of relationships. But in Joshua Achan confesses his sin (apparently wholeheartedly and genuinely) and yet it does not avert his death (Josh. 7:19–26).[8] So, on the one hand, Joshua is an Old Testament text that might, rather surprisingly, have more Christian significance than many Old Testament texts owing to its desire prophetically to reshape the basic underlying ancient Israelite worldview as indicated in Rahab's story amongst others. But on the other hand, Joshua is a narrative that we cannot straightforwardly 'apply', such as is the case with the inability of Achan's confession to restore his situation and relationships. So we must be careful to understand what role the 'narrative concerns' are playing in the story, as well as considering how various aspects of the content of the narrative might or might not recede from view in the Christian use of the text as it is read in the light of further revelation. So, to take another example, we have seen that the extreme *herem* of Jericho serves the *literary function* of making the stories of Rahab and Achan work – it is not there to describe actual practice, either past or present. So we must be careful in seeking to read doctrine off the narrative in a straightforward way. We seek in vain for a set of hermeneutical rules that will automatically 'process' any text.

## The Interpretation of Joshua in the Christian tradition

How has Joshua actually been read in the Christian tradition? We have already noted the use of Rahab's story as exemplifying faithful response to God as one of the main ways of handling Joshua as Christian Scripture. This has its roots in the New Testament, for in Heb. 11:31 she is held up as a model of faith, and in Jas. 2:25 she provides an example of the necessity of faith being accompanied by, or embodied in works. But one of the major approaches to reading Joshua has been to read the book with reference to the idea of 'spiritual warfare'. For example, in a homily on Joshua Origen suggests that

> doubtless the wars that are waged through Jesus [Joshua], and the slaughter of kings and enemies must also be said to be 'a shadow and type of heavenly things,' [Heb 8:5] namely, of those wars that our Lord Jesus with his army and officers – that is, the throngs of believers and their leaders – fights against the Devil and his angels. For it is he himself who strives with Paul and with the Ephesians 'against sovereigns and authorities and the rulers of darkness, against spiritual forces of wickedness in heavenly places.' [Eph. 6:12] . . . The kingdoms of earth are not promised to you by the gospels, but kingdoms of heaven. These kingdoms, however, are neither deserted nor abandoned; they have their own inhabitants, sinners and vile spirits, fugitive angels. Paul, sounding the apostolic trumpet, exhorts you to the battle against those who dwell there. Just as Jesus said then that your war would be against the Amorites and Perizzites and Hivites and Jebusites, likewise Paul also declares to you here, saying, 'Your fight will not be against flesh and blood,'

that is, we shall not fight in the same manner as the ancients fought. Nor are the battles in our land to be conducted against humans 'but against sovereigns, against authorities, against the rulers of darkness of this world.' [Eph. 6:12] Certainly you understand now where you must undertake struggles of this kind.[9]

This sort of reading is typical of the way that Joshua has often been read in a Christian context. Another kind of traditional approach to Joshua is reflected in Calvin's *Institutes* in which entrance to the Promised Land is a 'type' or 'shadow' for the Christian future inheritance:

> But in Scripture sometimes God, in conferring all these earthly benefits on them, determined to lead them by his own hand to the hope of heavenly things . . . [I]n the earthly possession [the Israelites] enjoyed, they looked, as in a mirror, upon the future inheritance they believed to have been prepared for them in heaven.[10]

Given that the language of warfare in Joshua 1 is transformed into a picture that is evocative of the nature of obedience to the law of Moses, and given the importance of 'rest' and the fulfilment of promise in Joshua (e.g. Josh. 1:15; 11:23 and 21:43–45), then in a sense these readings of Origen and Calvin are readings that explore the plenitude of the symbolic nature of Joshua that is fitting with respect to both the text of Joshua and its concerns, and to Joshua as a part of the canon of Scripture. In other words Origen's reading is a fairly natural kind of way of trying to develop Joshua 1 when it is read alongside Eph 6:10–18, and Calvin's reading is a natural way of reading Joshua as being part of our story as Christians.

However, in terms of the reading of Joshua developed in chapter 4, although these are possible ways of using the text of Joshua, they may be somewhat peripheral ways of exploring the text in terms of what the book of Joshua actually sought to achieve. Focusing on the text in the ways that Origen or Calvin do can lead one to miss the point of what Joshua is really about even as they explore imaginative ways of reading the text in a

Christian context. In other words, we need to go back to the text itself and consider what it was crafted to achieve in order to consider whether and how the story may be used in a robustly fitting way in the Christian context today as it is read alongside and through other myths that shape Christian identity so that the plenitude of the text may be explored responsibly and well, i.e. in a way that is fitting with respect to the text and with respect to the Christian tradition and with respect to the contemporary context. So what was Joshua primarily intended to achieve, and how might (or might not) this develop and be expressed in the Christian context? How might the Christian tradition illuminate Joshua, and conversely, how might Joshua illuminate the Christian tradition?

## Taking the tradition forward

As a starting point I would like to take the extended narrative of the crossing of the Jordan in Joshua 3–4 and develop its Christian use in the light of what we find in the remainder of Joshua using traditional Christian readings of this momentous event. In a sense I think that the traditional Christian reading of Joshua 3–4 that associates the Jordan crossing with baptism is along the right lines. However, the way that the association is understood needs to be developed in ways that are more evocative and symbolic than strictly 'typological'. Moreover, the way that such a symbolic reading, of using the Jordan crossing to evoke baptism, then relates to the book as a whole needs closer attention than it has usually been given. Let us start with J. Daniélou's discussion of the Jordan crossing in Gregory of Nyssa's mystical writings:

> Gregory's doctrine on baptism makes use of the various biblical types, especially the crossing of the Red Sea. In another image which he uses we find the River Jordan considered as one of the rivers of Paradise, and this symbolism stresses the idea of rebirth – baptism is thus represented as a return to the Garden of Eden. The entrance into the baptistery means that 'the Garden of Paradise and, indeed, heaven itself is once again

accessible to man' and that 'the sword of flame no longer prevents his approach.' . . . Again, the Jordan is considered as a figure of Baptism in the traditional way, as for example, by reference to the cure of Naaman the leper, or to the entrance of the Jews into the Promised Land.

> Cross the Jordan, [he says,] hasten towards the new life in Christ, to the land that bears fruit in happiness, flowing with milk and honey according to the promise. Overthrow Jericho, your former way of life! . . . All these things are figures of the reality which is now made manifest. [*Against those who put off Baptism* (PG 46.421A)]

But what is original with Gregory is the linking of the Jordan with the Garden of Eden. Taking up an idea which seems to have been first developed by the Gnostics, Gregory contrasts the rivers that flow down from Paradise with the Jordan, which flows back to heaven and has its source in Christ.

> Hurry to my Jordan, not at the call of John, but at the command of Christ. For the river of grace does not rise in Palestine and flow into the nearby sea, but flows everywhere, circling the entire world, and empties into Paradise. For it flows in a different direction from those four streams which flow from Eden and bears a cargo much more precious than that which was borne out by them. . . . For it brings back those who have been reborn by the Spirit. [*Against those who put off Baptism* (PG 46.420C)]

The true Jordan that covers the entire world is the water of Baptism, consecrated by the Baptism of Christ, and it grows into an immense stream which carries men back to Paradise.[11]

Going back to what we discovered in chapter 4, the crossing of the Jordan into the land was, for Joshua, symbolic of entrance into the fullness of life with God as symbolized by the covenant and the promised land. To 'cross the Jordan' was to cross into life, an understanding reflected in the Dead Sea

Scrolls text the 'Community Rule', 1QS. So to see the Jordan crossing as symbolizing baptism – which marks the symbolic entry into the Christian life – is a powerfully evocative and fitting way of reading the text in a Christian context. Such an interpretation respects what the narrative symbolism sought to achieve in its original context whilst re-expressing it in the language of a new context. In other words, the symbol of Jordan crossing is related to 'supernaturally' crossing into life – God extends what is humanly possible in drawing sinners into the newness and abundance of Christian life.

But how then does such an interpretation fit with the overall story of Joshua? I think that traditional readings have often been disappointing in that they fail to take this next step, to consider how this way of reading Joshua 3–4 then relates to the way in which the story proceeds in Joshua. I suggest that Joshua is concerned with developing just what entrance into this new life might involve in terms of what makes up 'true Israel' and how 'true Israel' might relate to 'non-Israel', and in particular, how the form of life envisaged here in Joshua might differ somewhat from that envisaged in Deuteronomy 7. What is to characterize those who enter into this life and live it? How are those living this life to relate to others who in varying degrees do or do not live (or wish to live) a similar kind of life? These, I suggest, are the very things that Joshua is concerned with – what it sought to achieve as discourse. So a Christian use of Joshua will be concerned with how these questions might be tackled in a Christian context. In other words, to enter into new life by going through the waters of baptism involves entering into a community that is characterized by certain attitudes and practices and types of relationships with others.

Let us recap on what we saw was going on in Joshua. The stories in Joshua 2 and 6–12 are built around the portrayal of *herem* in various ways. In a sense, in the 'world of the text', *herem* symbolizes 'divine action in the world' as mediated through human practice. But the stories relate in different ways to response-to-*herem*, which symbolically reflects response-to-God. So how one responds to *herem* in the world of the text reflects how one responds to what 'God is doing' thus indicating how one responds to God. Rahab (Joshua 2 and 6), when confronted with the campaign of *herem*, responds with *hesed* and glorifies God. She is thereby established as one who responds faithfully to God, despite appearances (being the Canaanite prostitute). Achan, on the other hand (Josh. 7), when confronted with the *herem* command at Jericho covets and steals. His response to *herem* establishes him as one who, despite appearances (the genealogical Israelite), responds unfaithfully to God. On the other hand Joshua and the Israelites are portrayed as being obedient to *herem* commands, symbolizing obedience to God, despite the ethical risks and difficulties that this portrayal creates at the level of the narrative. Conversely, the hostile kings respond with aggression toward Israel when confronted by God as symbolized by *herem* in the world of the text (Josh. 10:1–5 and 11:1–5), establishing themselves as being those who respond unfaithfully to God. In other words, confrontation with *herem* symbolizes confrontation with God in the world of the text and provides a 'test' that reflects the question of who is truly of the nature of Israel and who is not, challenging Deuteronomy 7:1–5 in this regard, since Deuteronomy 7:1–5 implied that there was nobody of the nature of Israel outside what was apparently Israel.

But Joshua goes beyond simply offering a new set of criteria to 'test' whether or not one has the character of 'Israel', for the story of the Gibeonites seems to blur even the notion of a straightforward test. Their story seems to be deliberately ambiguous. But when we reach the conclusion of Joshua in Joshua 23–24, we see that Joshua does not wish to reject Deuteronomy 7. Rather, Joshua wishes to qualify and nuance what Deuteronomy 7 expresses – separation from non-Israel so as not to be led astray into idolatry, but separation of a slightly different nature according to slightly different criteria. Remember that we saw that Joshua 23 reinforced the idea of separation that we found as central to Deuteronomy 7. In Joshua 23 it is still the case that Israel was not to intermarry or make covenants with non-Israelites. But Joshua has redefined the idea of what it is that makes up an Israelite – out are the Achans and the aggressive locals, but in are the Rahabs and the faithful, obedient Israelites. In other words, the idea of being 'out' or 'in', and the idea of separation finds symbolic expression in the narratives of Joshua. Separation from the outsider finds symbolic expression at the narrative level in death (the ultimate form of separation) (Josh. 7:25–26), whilst incorporation into the community finds expression in terms of living 'in the midst' of Israel for the insider (Josh. 6:25).

So what Joshua seems to be seeking to achieve is, on the one hand, to reinforce much of what Deuteronomy has to say regarding faithful response to God. Faithful response is embodied in faithfully living out the law of Moses (*torah*) (Josh. 1), glorifying God and living a life of *hesed*. And, according to Joshua 23, faithful response to God also involves separation from 'non-Israel' (now redefined) so as to avoid idolatry. But on the other hand Joshua qualifies the notion of just who might count as truly Israel or non-Israel, and to make decisions as to who counts as in or out near the boundary demanding and difficult. Through the narratives of Joshua 6 – 11 and the conclusion of Joshua 24, Israel is characterized by those who respond positively and faithfully to the God, choosing to serve God. Joshua challenges notions of identity that are based on certain established notions such as genealogy (Rahab, Achan) and geography (the transjordanians in Josh. 22).

Thus what we find in the narrative of Joshua then are ways in which certain aspects of the new life that is entered into by crossing the Jordan in Joshua 3–4 are given content in terms of what the sort of boundaries of the community that reflects this new life looks like, and what attitudes the community is to have to those inside and outside the community. Joshua expresses a new life that is demanding of those who count themselves as insiders (e.g. Achan), and exhibits an open-ness to those who are apparently outsiders, but actually manifest the characteristics of the insider. So the book gives content to how one understands the kind of community that one is 'crossing into'. This is where the classic association of the Jordan crossing with baptism needs to be developed, to say something about the sort of community that one is entering at baptism. By going through the waters of baptism one is entering into a community that is characterized by people who are

serious about living out their response to God in terms of obedience, glorifying God, demonstrating steadfast love and
avoiding idolatry and aggression. Joshua calls for the embrace
by the community of those whose lives reflect the former, positive characteristics, but for avoidance of those whose lives are
characterized by idolatry and aggression for example.

Whilst the accounts of land grant in Joshua 13–21 have
rather little continuing significance in the Christian context as
such, perhaps some of the stories that relate to the possessing
of the land might find some continued use. The characters in
these stories reflect the embodiment of what traits do, or do
not, indicate what is associated with possessing new life in the
land. We see in Caleb (Josh. 14:6–15) and in Achsah's daughter
(Josh. 15:13–19) the traits of boldness and initiative, for example, a boldness that stems from trust in God's promise.
Negatively, in the Josephites (Josh. 17:14–18) we find a lack of
courage and zeal, something that seems to reflect a failure to
act boldly in the light of God's promise. These stories together
with Joshua 6–11 indicate what it is that is to characterize one
who responds to God well.

But are these concerns alien to the New Testament? Taking
Joshua 13–21 first, the idea of boldness as characterizing a
desirable form of response to God is something that has
important resonances with certain aspects of the the Christian
concept of faith. Indeed, the notion of boldness gives content
to what faith 'looks like' (cf. Luke 11:8; Acts 4:13, 29; Heb. 4:16).
But turning to the rest of Joshua, we find many of the very
sorts of idea introduced above reflected and carried through
into the New Testament. In John's gospel in particular it is
Jesus who reflects the supreme instance of 'divine action in the
world'. One's identity, in relation to the Christian community,
is indicated by how one responds to him. As *herem* involves the
idea of division, so Jesus brings division (cf. Luke 12:51) –
when one encounters Jesus one must respond, and such a
response is in a sense an act of self-judgment, an act of self-
determination of one's identity, even as it is a response that is
enabled by grace. Moreover, the gospels pose challenging and
unsettling questions of identity. The question of who it is that
truly 'sees', and thus responds appropriately to Jesus, and who

it is that is in fact blind resounds through the gospels, especially in John and Mark. Those who are apparently blind, or
the outcasts, 'see', whilst the insiders who claim to see, such as
the Pharisees, are in fact blind and fail to 'see' and are unable
to respond appropriately to Jesus. In this sense similar concerns pervade Joshua and the gospels. They are both concerned with redefining how the community understands its
identity as shaped in response to God as expressed in response
to Jesus (in the case of the gospels), and what this means,
something that will entail surprising qualifications or even
reversals of cherished ideas.

However, in another sense there are important differences,
for as we have seen, the New Testament is concerned with
transformation in a way that often the Old Testament is not,
and so the Christian community is concerned with an incar-
nate mission to idolatrous and aggressive outsiders, rather
than separation from them. Whilst Christians are to seek to
separate themselves from idolatry, the Christian community is
not to be one segregated from the world, in one sense at least.
Moreover, as Christians we are simultaneously 'saints' and
'sinners' (expressing the idea of mediation, i.e., sharing in two
categories as per neo-structuralist vocabulary), so the question
of 'separation' from idolaters and indeed idolatry in the life of
the Christian needs careful formulation.[12] In summary then, it
seems that some aspects of the life entered into on baptism do
reflect what Joshua envisages, whilst others differ, such as the
nature of separation and (more obviously) the role of *torah* obedience, which is re-expressed in terms of obedience to Jesus,
owing to the 'oldness' of the Old Covenant that results from
the Incarnation and God's desire to draw all people into relationship with him through Christ.

Thus, to develop a point made by Nicholas Lash,[13] the
Christian interpreter of Joshua is not first and foremost to be
concerned with questions such as, 'How might or ought
Christians practise *herem* today?', even in the symbolic sense
that we have developed. Rather, the concern should be to consider how what Joshua 'intended, showed or achieved'
through the symbolic use of *herem*, might be re-expressed
today in concrete forms of practice and behaviour in the light

of new revelatory myths (such as those that the Incarnation gives birth to), and in the light of our concrete context and its concerns (such as the problem of genocide and religiously motivated violence in the 20th and early 21st centuries). In other words, how might faithful response to divine action in the world today be mapped out in the light of what Joshua had to say about faithful response to God in such a way as to allow for the potential 'oldness' (and so possible 'obsolescence') of some aspects of Joshua, but also to allow Joshua's 'own voice' to be preserved and heard and not have a later voice simply imposed rather awkwardly on it?

## Reading Joshua alongside the gospels

It might be helpful to think about how one might use Joshua to illuminate some of the stories in the gospels that relate to challenging questions regarding insiders and outsiders. In other words, we can consider how to use Joshua to help us to read the New Testament, rather than simply seeking to read the New Testament back into the Old. Some of the gospel stories are actually rather challenging when one thinks about what they say about faithful response to God. The story about the Canaanite (or Syro-Phoenician) woman (Matt. 15:21–28) has certain similarities to Rahab's story. Here, a Canaanite woman (and thus apparently an outsider) demonstrates great faith, and is an example to the insider on the nature of faith (15:28). Alternatively, the parable of the sheep and the goats (Matt 25:31–46) offers a challenging reflection on the nature of the recognition of Jesus and of adequate response to him. Similarly Matthew 7:21–23 offers another demanding reflection on the nature of response to Jesus, and one that is particularly challenging to some contemporary forms of evangelical and charismatic spirituality in particular. Here, one might say that it is not the 'sinner's prayer' or the exercise of a spectacular charismatic ministry that is said to be at the heart of what marks out the true follower of Jesus. Rather, the true insider, the true follower of Jesus is one who at heart 'does the will of the Father' (Matt. 7:21). The ability to prophesy, the ability to cast out demons, and the ability to perform other miracles is, Jesus says, of little consequence in demonstrating a Christian identity and thus faithful response to Jesus in comparison with 'doing the will of the Father'.

So these stories that we find in Matthew have much in common with what we find in Joshua. The narratives are tackling the question of what makes for faithful response to God and what it is that characterizes the insider, often in surprising ways. In the same way that Achan is seen to be complacent of his identity as an Israelite owing to his ethnicity, a complacency that indicates that he is not a true Israelite at all, Matthew suggests that those who are complacent of their Christian identity in some sense – in those who base their identity solely on the 'sinner's prayer', the exercise of charismatic gifts, or the practise of love only when it is visibly and explicitly 'for Jesus' – risk being no Christians at all.

However, if we just read these passages in Matthew we might come away thinking that the Christian life is all about 'works' in some way – another premature drawing of the boundary of the community and resolution of Christian identity perhaps. 'Works' might be seen as the essential basis of Christian identity. But turning to Luke's gospel, we see that there is a refusal to make this move. For example, in the parable of the Pharisee and the tax collector (Luke 18:9–14), we find that it is not works but a recognition of sin leading to a plea for mercy that makes up faithful response to God, rather like the 'sinner's prayer'. Likewise there is the famous account of the thief on the cross next to Jesus who simply asks Jesus to remember him (Luke 23:39–43). Again, for Luke this plea would seem to encapsulate faithful response to Jesus.

So read together, the gospels, rather like Joshua, seem to want to make it difficult for us to 'pin down' precisely what marks out being a part of God's people as a Christian.[14] The problem is that this is what we want to do so much of the time, to have a 'formula' that establishes what makes up Christian identity. But a careful reading of the gospels, as might be motivated by a reading of Joshua, shows that this is something to be refused. By analogy then, the story of Rahab indicates that there may be those who are seemingly 'un-Christian' but who might in fact be as much Christian as the model Christian, as we would think of them. The story of Achan shows that there are those who are apparently model Christians but who may in fact be unconverted in the heart. Together, these stories reverse expectations (rather like Luke's parable of the Pharisee and the tax collector) about what it might mean to be a Christian. But just in case we might be tempted to think that we can establish a new set of criteria for 'membership' in the Christian community, the story of the Gibeonites in Joshua indicates that the boundaries will be 'fuzzy' and impossible to draw. The inclusion of both Matthew and Luke in the canon alongside each other with their differing perspectives on what constitutes faithful response to God indicates that in the Christian context we need to preserve a sense of this difficulty in trying to define faithful response to God – we must retain a sense of mystery in the presence of God, that it is God who defines and draws his community to himself.

Finally, this 'problematizing' of the essence of identity is indicated in a different way in another interesting story in Joshua – the transjordanians and their altar in Joshua 22. Here is another example of expected perspectives being reversed, with cherished ideas of the essence of identity being qualified. Here, life in the land west of the Jordan is shown as not being finally determinative of Israelite identity. But what is interesting is that there is a mistaking of the symbol for the reality demonstrated in the story. Life in the land *symbolizes* life in covenant with God, but it is not finally *equated* with that life, even though it embodies it and shares in it. Indeed, one aspect of myth and symbol that we considered earlier was the tendency for the symbol or myth to 'collapse' into the 'literal sense' in which it simply becomes a description of things. The symbol is equated with 'reality', or with 'history' in the case of Joshua, with it being seen as a text describing genocide. What is interesting is that Joshua itself anticipates this kind of problem, especially in the story of Joshua 22 where caution is urged in not mistaking the symbol of the land for the 'reality' that it expresses, i.e., life in covenant and blessing with the Lord. The symbol is not to be confused with the reality. And perhaps we tend to do this in the Christian context where we mistake symbols of the Christian life for the life, or what the symbols point to, itself.

## Joshua and openness to 'the other'

Joshua is a difficult and demanding text, but not in the ways that we have come to see it as being difficult. The use of the story of Rahab is a good example, for the significance of her story has often been expressed in terms of her faith and her 'conversion'. In a sense this is a good way of reading the text in the Christian context, but in a sense it is also to *miss* the main point of the story. The text of Joshua is not concerned with Rahab's 'conversion' at all – she is simply presented as one who, through *hesed* and glorifying the Lord, *already* manifests the identity of the 'true Israelite'. In other words, the story is not about her conversion. So why is her story seen in terms of conversion? Well, it is a conversion story, but it is not a story of Rahab's conversion. Rather, her story is a story that urges the conversion of the perception of Israel towards some of those who are regarded as outside Israel by Israel, as seen in the conversion of Israel's own understanding expressed in Deuteronomy 7. Rahab's story is thus first and foremost a challenge to the 'conversion' of the insider, and not the outsider. In Christian terms, her story is a challenge to the conversion of the attitude of the church to those apparently outside what one thinks of as church – it is certainly an ecumenical text. The demanding edge of the story has been lost if we take the story of Rahab as referring to *Rahab's* conversion. It is a story that challenges the church and those within the church, when read in the Christian context, and not the unconverted. The reading perspective for the story is, therefore, crucial. This is why certain types of postcolonial readings of the story in which Rahab is viewed only in terms of a Canaanite perspective and context go astray. But ironically, when Joshua is read well from the perspective of being inside the community that it addresses, rather than outside (as per postcolonialist readings), Rahab's story does encourage certain aspects of postcolonialist ideology, especially when read alongside Joshua 5:13–15. That is, Joshua refuses the simple categorization of a 'them' and an 'us', encouraging an openness to the outsider and a self-critique of the insider,[15] something that is obscured if Joshua is read from a Canaanite perspective in which Rahab is simply seen as a traitor for instance.

Perhaps it is worth dwelling on Joshua 5:13–15 for a while, and the theological implications that it might have. Here a mysterious figure who subsequently identifies himself as the commander of the Lord's army appears with a drawn sword before Joshua. Joshua asks him if he is 'for us or for our adversaries', a question that the commander refuses with the cryptic answer 'no' (some translations have 'neither' at this point). Joshua falls face down in reverence and removes his sandals following the commander's instruction. And this ends the encounter. What is the significance of this little account? Taking a step back for a moment, perhaps a difficulty with the sort of reading of Joshua that I am proposing is that it seems like, or it may become, simply another ideology competing with other ideologies in contemporary society – one of a certain kind of 'openness' to the 'other'. In many ways this might be seen as an ideology that sits well in today's society – Rahab's story might be seen as indicative of a general air of 'tolerance' for example. But this is not quite what Joshua is doing. Whilst an openness to the outsider is encouraged, it is an *openness based on a certain kind of responsiveness to God in the outsider that is difficult and demanding*. I think that what is encapsulated in Joshua 5:13–15 is a refusal of the idea of drawing ideologies 'from below', as it were, and seeking to co-opt God into them. The commander of the Lord's army refuses to 'take sides' as they might be humanly constructed. That is, the commander of the Lord's army, representing God, refuses to be co-opted to the interests of one group and its own ideology as it conceives it, or another. What Joshua 5:13–15 indicates is a transcending of this kind of perspective to a response to God in worship. This suggests that the makeup of the community of those who are truly in relationship with God (i.e., those for whom God is 'for us') is something that comes from beyond us, from beyond any humanly constructed community and its own ideology. That is, the community of those in relationship with God is something that is constructed by God, according to God's perspective, in grace. We see this worked out in the stories that follow – God is 'with' or 'for' those who respond well to him, as symbolized by *herem*. God is 'for' Rahab but not Achan. So Joshua 5:13–15 does not encourage one to view

Joshua as simply a reflection of yet another competing ideology in the world. Joshua 5:13–15 reflects an attempt to move beyond competing ideologies. It is an ideology – theology in fact – that comes 'from beyond' as grace. If there is a 'delusion' in Joshua it is here, in Joshua's assumption that God can be co-opted onto sides, a 'delusion' that the book Joshua corrects.

## Joshua and genocide

But what about the question of genocide? It is interesting that traditionally Joshua has been read in spiritual terms, relating more to the 'battles' of the spiritual life than to questions of actual warfare or conquest, as we saw in Origen's reading above. The same can be said about Deuteronomy 7:1–5 – in the mediaeval work the *glossa ordinaria* for example the 'seven nations' are interpreted allegorically as the seven main vices that the 'spiritual warrior' overcomes by God's grace. I think that this traditional instinct is basically correct in that it has been recognized that Joshua, and Deuteronomy 7:1–5, are not actually 'about' genocide or violence. Indeed, I have said very little about how Joshua relates to warfare and violence thus far. And this is deliberate, not because I wish to dodge the issue, but because I have wished to show that these issues are really not what Joshua is concerned with. Perhaps a helpful analogy is to consider the film 'Titanic' – whilst the film is set in the context of the maiden voyage of the Titanic, it is not really about the Titanic and its maiden voyage. Rather, it is really a tragic love story.[16] Joshua is a story set in the context of genocide, but it is not about genocide, either as a description of what happened in the distant past, or as something that is in any sense a model to be followed or glorified in. Joshua wished to challenge some of the assumptions of Deuteronomy 7, even though Deuteronomy 7 is not really about genocide either, but separation and segregation as we have seen. But Joshua used the very language and symbolism of *herem* in Deuteronomy 7 in a new, imaginative way to qualify some of Deuteronomy 7's assumptions. Joshua is a discourse that challenges from within, adopting the preferred vocabulary of those Joshua wishes to challenge.

So the questions that the interpreter who wishes to understand the book of Joshua (and indeed Deut. 7) may reasonably ask from the text are not those 'historical' questions concerning how Israel entered in to or emerged as a nation in the Promised Land, nor what methods of warfare might or might not have used by ancient Israelites. These may be interesting and proper questions for the historian, but these questions were simply not in view for the book of Joshua – it is concerned with questions that are altogether different.

But what about the portrait of God that Joshua seems to imply? Some of the most challenging and difficult parts of the narrative are those that directly implicate God in *herem*, in that Israel was acting obediently to God in carrying out what we would term genocide. The difficulty here is the assumption that we can read something of the nature of God off such reports in the narrative such as Joshua 10:40. But if, as we have seen, the narrative works more subtly than simply offering a description of things, then it is perilous to assume that one can simply 'read off' what God is like from the story. Indeed, we have seen that it is perilous to try and read doctrine or history off the narrative in a straightforward way, for elements in the story may serve a variety of ends. So the report of obedience to God in 10:40 may in fact serve to give warrant not to genocide, but rather to the kind of reshaping of the self-understanding of the community of Israel as achieved through the stories of Rahab, Achan and the Gibeonites for example. In other words, what the report of 10:40 might suggest, albeit rather subtly, is that the way that Rahab, Achan and the Gibeonites were treated won divine approval.

Thus one *need not* say that the Israelites 'got it wrong' in their perception of God, because the narrative might not be trying to make statements about the nature of God in the same way as it might not be trying to make historical statements. Neither does one need to appeal to an apologetic of 'total depravity' to suppose that all people are guilty sinners by nature and deserve death, and thus that the Canaanites deserved their fate, in order to try and 'redeem' the narrative. Indeed, the narrative of Joshua makes nothing of the sinfulness or depravity of the local inhabitants. Nor does one need to appeal to the notion of a 'different God' from the God of the New Testament, nor indeed to a dispensational account of the nature of God – that God displayed wrath long ago and that he will display such wrath again, but not now (so much).[17]

So I hope that it has become clear that Joshua really has nothing to say regarding the conduct of war, either for ancient Israel or for us today. Joshua does not offer a blueprint for colonialism, nor does it offer a blueprint for the postcolonial rejection of such narratives. Neither does Joshua provide guidance for the legitimacy of certain kinds of practice of warfare, such as the use of ambush (Josh. 8), a concern that was important in the Christian use of this particular text. As we have seen in other examples, this is a case of a narrative level theme that serves the interests of the story (here, I think by making the story a more interesting and exciting story) rather than being a source of ethics or history.

But perhaps there is still the question of the use of symbols that convey violence and warfare. In a sense, I do not wish to push the apologetic side of my reading too far – I think that Israel did consider that Yahweh 'fought' on her behalf, and I think that we still think of God fighting on our behalf as Christians today, even if not so much in the realm of actual physical warfare. There are two points to consider here. First, it seems that if there is no realm of human activity where God is not present, nowhere that we can flee from God, then in a sense God must be 'involved' somehow in all human conflict and warfare, even if the questions of where and how are ambiguous, something that Joshua 5:13–15 already suggests.[18] However, as I said above, I do not think that Joshua provides us with the material to address these questions – they need to be tackled from elsewhere. Secondly, the image or metaphor of 'fighting' is, I think, an important one for saying something about the nature of the Christian life, as is indicated in much traditional Christian reading of Joshua. Indeed, in various contexts and traditions the idea of 'spiritual warfare' keeps resurfacing. So I do not think that we need to reject the metaphors of fighting, battle and warfare for they provide an important resource for the Christian life, even if it is important that their metaphorical nature be recognized.[19] However, yet again, I do

not think that Joshua has much to say on these issues, apart
from the note in Joshua 1 on the importance of being bold and
strong in *torah* obedience, which Christians might interpret as
being strong in obedience to Christ – in living the Christian
life.

## Summary

What I have been trying to show in reading Joshua as myth is
how to reclaim an understanding of what the text actually 'is'
– what its genre is if you like, and how it might be used well in
the Christian context. This means that we will want to read
Joshua in different ways from those to which we have become
accustomed to once we understand the nature of the material.
It is not, I suggest, about portraying history, and it is not about
providing a metaphysical description of the nature of God.
This is not to say that history and the nature of God are unimportant to Joshua. Joshua arises out of the history of a tradition
that embodies responsiveness to God's calling and seeks,
prophetically, to shape a history 'in front of the text' of faithful
response to God, saying something about God implicitly, but
not quite in the way that is sometimes assumed.

Joshua is not about genocide. Rather Joshua seeks to evoke
something of the nature of what life in the community of
God's people looks like, in terms of the nature of relationships
with others on the one hand, and loving, bold, faithful obedience on the other. There are some similarities and some differences in the way that these concerns work out in practice in
daily life for the Christian, with the form of Rahab's response
being developed into a model for Christian responsiveness to
God on the one hand, but the form of response to aggressive,
idolatrous outsiders being transformed from one of separation
to one of mission. Joshua undergoes transformation as it is
read in new contexts, as myths do generally, with the forms of
transformation being illuminated by neo-structuralism.

# 6.

# So what?

The sort of reading of Joshua that I am proposing is perhaps something of a double-edged sword for many Christians – something that I feel myself. On the one hand, in our contemporary context in which genocide and religiously motivated violence are, sadly, all too familiar, with the Old Testament being something of an embarrassing 'no go area' for many Christians owing to its apparent collusion with genocide, a reading like the one proposed here might provide a renewed way of engaging wholeheartedly with our more difficult yet nonetheless cherished texts. But on the other hand, a reading like the one presented here is likely to be worrying for many Christians for a number of reasons. First, because we are so accustomed to thinking in terms of the correspondence between 'history' and 'truth', to argue that Joshua is not 'history' may be troubling, especially when Joshua is apparently part of a larger 'historical scheme' in the Bible. Indeed, Joshua understood 'as history' perhaps represents an important building block of what might be termed 'salvation history'. Secondly, I think that particularly in Evangelical traditions Scripture tends to be regarded as being straightforward to interpret, and reading in the way that I suggest makes interpretation seem like a rather difficult affair in which one needs a good deal of help from 'experts'. Thirdly, drawing these two concerns together, to say that the narrative of Joshua is not to be understood in terms of God '*historically* saying this' or '*historically* doing this' – as various statements imply, when taken at face value – may be seen as the thin end of the wedge, a 'selling out' to a 'liberal' or 'anti-supernatural' worldview perhaps.


## Joshua and history

But what are the implications of my approach to Joshua? Let us start by thinking about the question of 'history', and of what my proposed reading of Joshua might suggest. The reading that I am proposing does not find Joshua's significance in terms of the report of a 'history' of how Israel entered the Promised Land as such. Rather, Joshua is primarily an engaging story that seeks to shape the identity of Israel in new forms of ever more faithful response to God. The story may or may not have strong links with actual historical events. Joshua is, therefore, concerned with 'history' more in the sense that it seeks to shape the 'history' of a people 'in front of the text' (that is, it 'wants' to shape the ongoing 'histories' of its readers and the community it is addressed to), rather than report the history of a past people 'behind the text'. In other words, Joshua 'seeks' to *create* history rather than to *report* it – a prophetic text perhaps, in the sense that it calls forth a response in the way that one lives. But this is not to say that there is or is not a 'historical core' to Joshua in some sense. Minimally, there is a historical core in the sense that Israel emerged as a nation who possessed (to varying degree) the Promised Land and worshipped the Lord in covenant there. But would one want to say more than this? I think that the question of whether or not there was a 'historical conquest' cannot be settled using the book of Joshua – I think that this question needs to be tackled on other grounds. It may be that agnosticism on this issue is wise.

I do not wish to argue that Israel did not engage in warfare and battle. Israel's identity as a nation was shaped by her emergence from various conflicts. She fought wars just like nations have throughout history, and sought to discern the presence of God in such warfare, just as we find in other ancient Near Eastern (and contemporary) accounts of war. I do not wish to argue that Israel was a pacifist nation, or that she understood her response to God in pacifist terms. Rather, what I wish to show is that the portrayals of genocide that we find in the Old Testament are not functioning as historical descriptions of genocide or conquest, and hence that one cannot infer from such portrayals that God is perceived as commanding or condoning genocide. Rather, as we have seen, such portrayals serve symbolic or literary functions in ways that I have attempted to demonstrate.

Turning to the questions of ethics and how these work out in relation to portrayals of genocide in the Old Testament, in this book I have only considered Joshua and Deuteronomy 7 in any detail as these are, I think, the main and most problematic accounts relating to genocide. But I think that similar literary or symbolic readings are appropriate for other accounts in the Old Testament. For example, 1 Samuel 15 is the only other extended account that deals with *herem* in the Old Testament. Here Saul is ordered, through Samuel the prophet, to 'utterly destroy' (*herem*) the Amalekites, including children and animals, rather like the order of the extreme *herem* of Jericho. Now Saul destroys the Amalekites, but spares the best of the animals. In a sense then, he acts rather like Achan in Joshua 7, keeping the best of the spoils. In Joshua 7 such disobedience to God led to Achan's death. Here in 1 Samuel 15 this disobedience leads to Saul's rejection as king. In other words the 'extreme *herem*' here would seem to serve as a 'test' in the 'world of the text' in a very similar way to the way in which it serves as a test in Joshua. How one responds to *herem* represents a test that reflects (symbolically) how one responds to God. Moreover, the Amalekites are something of a 'mythical group' that personify evil in the Old Testament in much the same way that the Anakim (Anakites) and Rephaim (Rephaites) do in Joshua. In other words, it seems that the same sort of thing is going on here in 1 Samuel 15 as is going on in Joshua. *Herem* does not reflect 'what happened' but is functioning symbolically and mythically to make another point, i.e. testing faithful responsiveness to God in obedience, something that is made clear in the story itself (15:22). But as in Joshua, the narrative in 1 Samuel 15 does not suggest that obedient response to God on the part of the reader is actually to be shown in the practice of *herem* in the real world (remember Victor Turner's comments on myth). *Herem* is a symbolic test of obedience in the world of the text indicating extreme obedience. The *herem* narratives are not concerned with the practice or ethics of *herem* as it might be understood at face value, but rather with questions of obedience to God in demanding circumstances, and its testing.

Consider another example of an ethically difficult narrative, this time from 1 Samuel 27–30. In those chapters king David is reported as attacking and plundering various areas and as leaving no survivors (although his actions are not described in terms of *herem*. 1 Sam 27:9). Traditionally, David has been understood as a 'role model' whose actions are generally interpreted in a positive light. However, in an interesting new reading of the story of David, John Van Seters has argued that these narratives are in fact designed to cast David's actions in a negative light in order to introduce more ambiguity into the character of David and into the institution of Davidic kingship. In other words, here is another story that appears at face value to be glorying in genocide, whilst in fact the story might have the very opposite message.

Genesis 34 provides another example of an ethically and morally difficult narrative. Here, following the rape of Dinah (one of Jacob's daughters) by Shechem, a Hivite, negotiations laced with deception take place leading to the slaughter of the Hivites by Levi and Simeon, two of Dinah's brothers, although the term *herem* is not used here. I have discussed this difficult story elsewhere,[1] and so I just wish to note here that again the story is not really concerned with slaughter. Rather, what the story is trying to do is to indicate the rejection of the possibility of intermarriage between Israel and 'non-Israel' in symbolic terms, thus saying something about the identity and nature of Israel. The story seeks to support the ethnic nature of Israel's identity, and thus the impossibility of mediation with or transformation of outsiders into Israel, unlike Joshua. It is for these reasons, and not the portraits of deception and violence *per se* that the story becomes obsolete in a Christian context in which, as we have seen, mediation and transformation are essential to the construction of Christian identity. Genesis

34 does indeed sit uneasily in a Christian context, but not only for the reasons that one might think. In fact, it sits uneasily with Joshua.

There are a number of other narratives in the Old Testament that raise difficult questions with regard to the portrayal of genocide, violence and deception which will not be discussed here. But I hope that by looking at some of the most difficult – Genesis 34, Deuteronomy 7, Joshua and 1 Samuel 15, it is possible to see that genocide, violence and deception are often not the concerns that drive such stories. The concerns of these stories look rather different from those that we have often assumed today. It may turn out that some narratives in the Old Testament remain deeply problematic. But it surely makes things look rather different in our contemporary situation to see that what is arguably the 'main' problematic narrative – Joshua – does not function in a way that is often assumed today, and that the same can be said for other narratives such as 1 Samuel 15.

In many ways with reports like Joshua 10:12–14, where the sun stands still, we can remain ambivalent on the 'history behind the text' if we wish. However, there are other narratives where a reading such as I am suggesting *requires* the text to be unhistorical (at least in part) if we are to deduce (or not to deduce) certain things about God. I.e. if the report that Joshua was obedient to God in committing genocide (to use our term) (10:40) is historically accurate and reflects the proper discernment of God's will, then one will imagine God as being rather different than if one takes this report to be 'unhistorical' and serving a different function in the narrative. In other words, being willing to abandon the cherished 'plain sense' of some Old Testament texts, something that has dominated the reading of Old Testament narrative from the Reformation onwards, leads us to see God in rather different (but hopefully more faithful) ways, for the texts do not give us straightforward descriptions of the nature of God, or descriptions that lead to easy deductions regarding the nature of God.

Similarly, neither then do many biblical texts function to offer, in any straightforward way, models for behaviour, models for Christian ethics, or a set of rules to live by when the narratives are read at face value. The texts simply function in a different way, as highlighted in our study of the neo-structuralist approach to myth and in Victor Turner's approach to myth. But what this means in practice is that a rather disconcerting new way of reading Scripture is required if we are to read it faithfully (although it is a way of reading that stands in continuity in a number of ways with traditional reading of Scripture). What is required is a certain 'crucifying' of our contemporary assumptions of the ways in which the biblical material speaks, perhaps allowing a greater space for the 'mystery' of the biblical texts, through a willingness to let go of the cherished plain sense of Scripture as a way of interpreting the *whole* Bible in order to follow Jesus.[2] All this is not to say that the narratives of the Old Testament do not provide any guidance on how to live. I have been arguing quite the opposite. But what I am saying is that the guidance that the narratives gesture towards is not something that is simply read off the surface of the narrative as it stands at face value – guidance for living is evoked through the symbolism and perhaps 'structural level' concerns of the narratives. This of course makes interpreting and using Scripture difficult – but then this is perhaps why teaching is regarded as a special gift in the New Testament and that few should presume the role (Eph. 4:11 and Jas. 3:1). We have come to assume, rather too readily perhaps, that Scripture is easy to interpret and teach. Scripture is not a simple handbook of morals and ethics.

Thus I have sympathy with Richard Dawkins when he says, after discussing Joshua, that 'My main purpose . . . has not been to show that we *shouldn't* get our morals from scripture (although that is my opinion). My purpose has been to demonstrate that we (and that includes most religious people) as a matter of fact *don't* get our morals from scripture.'[3] I suggest that Dawkins is *partially* correct on both counts, if when we talk about 'getting morals from scripture' we mean reading off moral practice from the literal sense of the text at face value. I contend that we *should* (and often, indeed we *do*) get our morals from Scripture, but in the more indirect way that I have been describing.[4] But, as I indicated in chapter 5, this process is further complicated for Old Testament narratives in the sense that they are read through the New, as Christians have recognized throughout the ages.

## Joshua and salvation history

What about the question of 'salvation history'? As I have indicated, I am moving beyond an ambivalence toward the historical value of *some* Old Testament narratives – myths are generally ambivalent to the question of history – toward an actual denial of their 'historicity' for literary, anthropological, theological and ethical reasons in certain cases such as in the book of Joshua.[5] I am not arguing that Israel was naïve with regard to history, or simply bad at reporting it, but that *some* of the texts of the Old Testament often had different concerns entirely.

Perhaps the problem is that we are so used to reading the Bible as 'history' in the modern, critical sense. And indeed such reading is, it would often seem, encouraged by the ordering of the narrative books of the Old Testament into what appears to be a unified narrative of Israel's history – the roots of our 'salvation history'. Indeed, Joshua seems to pick up the story from the end of Deuteronomy, and Judges picks up the story from Joshua, and so on. But Old Testament scholars have often noted the rather different portraits of Israel's early life in Joshua and Judges, suggesting that Judges offers a portrait that seems more credible in an archaeological perspective. I do not wish to engage this debate here. Rather, what I wish to note is the way in which the beginning of Judges seems to have been written deliberately to link, or indeed 'harmonize' these two stories. Scholars have noted that the material in Judges 1–2 is rather different from that in the remainder of the book, concluding that Judges 1–2 was written to link up and harmonize the stories of Joshua and Judges into a 'grand historical narrative'. It seems to me that both books are stories with concerns other than those of historical reporting, but here in Judges 1–2 we see an 'editorial' move that grants both books a more 'historical' flavour, especially when they are read in their canonical context in a 'history' that begins with Genesis. What impact does this 'move towards history' have on the reading that I am proposing, especially as it is usually the canonical collection that is taken to be revelatory and the authoritative witness to God? If my reading of Joshua is correct, then how does this square with this idea of the salvation history of Israel and hence the church by extension?

First, if Judges 1–2 does indeed represent an 'editing togeth-er' of Joshua and Judges into a more historical scheme, then this itself suggests that a grand historical scheme, salvation history if you like, is a concept that required discernment and emerged relatively late in the life of Ancient Israel. It seems that these stories of Joshua and Judges previously stood along-side each other with there being no real desire to combine them into a unified historical narrative. In other words, the idea of salvation history, if we might call it that, is an under-standing of God's mode of relationship with humanity that is only discerned gradually through prophetic insight. Salvation history is a concept that gradually emerged, and it might be said to be a concept that *symbolizes* the nature of God's rela-tionship with humanity, especially if the narratives that are drawn into the emergence of the idea are themselves mythical and symbolic. In other words, this is not to say that this is not a 'real' or 'true' way of speaking of God's relationship with the world, but rather that it has symbolic expression in the Bible and is not 'history' (in the modern sense) *per se*.

Secondly, if we return to the observations introduced in chapter 2 that myths and symbols tend to 'tire' over time, then one could suggest that what we see here is a 'tiring' of the myth of Joshua as it comes to be seen in increasingly 'histori-cal' terms. Perhaps something of its symbolic significance is lost, and its significance is drawn towards that of a 'literal his-tory'. And this may be true in part. Normally such 'tiring' is a bad thing, for the true significance of the symbolism is lost. What the mythical narrative was trying to do in terms of shap-ing the response of people becomes obscured or distorted, just as with much contemporary understanding of Joshua in which its significance is seen only in terms of a bloody history. But does this mean that the 'harmonizing' of Joshua and Judges into a continuous 'history' is a bad thing or necessarily a 'tir-ing' of the myths? At one level it could be. But at another level, the way that these stories are creatively combined 'in history' is itself revelatory and perhaps the mythical expression of an emerging concept of salvation history – that God has a 'plan' in his dealings with humanity, and that he leads, shapes and guides the lives of his people. So, if you like, this harmonization of the narratives is a move that is expressive of the plenitude of the worlds of the texts, and the combination of myths into new myths as they are read alongside each other and in terms of each other. In a sense it is us with our critical approach to history that causes the difficulty, and not the process of the combination of the texts themselves in this way.

However, perhaps this concern with 'salvation history' is in fact present in Joshua itself, for Joshua is concerned with interpreting the possession of the land as the fulfilment of God's promise (Josh. 21:43–45). In other words, whilst Joshua is not a 'history book' as such, it does indeed reflect a concern with God's establishment of a people whom he calls to himself in a historical dimension, understood in terms of promise and fulfilment. As the concept of salvation history emerges more strongly Joshua provides the traditional or perhaps confessional symbolic resources to speak of this emerging idea of salvation history – Joshua's story reflects what is available to talk about and make sense of the idea of salvation history, a story that the community knows and agrees. What develops in this process of the emerging idea of salvation history can rightly be said to be revelatory, and a process that is prophetic, as new insight is gained into the nature of the relationship between God and the world.

But need the relationship between the events portrayed in the book of Joshua and actual events matter for the concept of salvation history to be a good and accurate one, as it is usually developed? I do not think that such a relationship is crucial, for what is important is that Israel *has* emerged as a nation, and that God *has* been instrumental in this process, and that Israel *has* discerned that this process is the result of Yahweh's calling of her as a nation. Whether this process, of the establishment of the nation Israel, was one of conquest of the Promised Land by a group of people (the Israelites) who had left Egypt (as per the biblical story taken at face value), or one of peasants who emerged as the nation Israel by rising up against oppressive overlords within Canaan (so Mendenhall and later Gottwald), or indeed a process of 'peaceful infiltration' (so Alt and Noth),[6] would seem not to matter here, for what is important is that God has in fact called and established *this* group of people in *this* land worshipping him through torah.

## Joshua and miracles

Perhaps another question that then arises is the significance of how God is portrayed more generally in the Old Testament, and whether he is primarily known in and through 'miracles' (as it is common to assume), such as in the crossing of the Jordan (Joshua 3–4) or in the stopping of the sun (Josh 10:12–14), particularly when the rhetoric of the texts themselves, and of the psalms, for example, talks up the importance of the 'deeds of the Lord' (e.g. Ps. 66:3). We have already discussed the symbolic nature of the narrative in Joshua, but what about the reception of such narratives in the psalms? Much of the language of the psalms is poetic liturgy that expresses, often in metaphorical ways, something of the relationship between God and the worshipper. The psalms provide a common language that worshippers can share in to   celebrate what the Lord has done, allowing the worshippers to speak intelligibly to each other about the Lord and about knowing him for the edification and growth of the worshipper and the worshipping community. As can be seen in Psalm 66, the language of God's 'awesome deeds', such as crossing the river on foot (66:6) is used to lead into the language of personal encounter with God. The general language of the 'deeds of the Lord' becomes a way of envisaging the sort of thing that God does 'for me', and for considering what implications this has for my response to God (66:16–20). The 'deeds of the Lord' such as the crossing of the Jordan provide powerful symbols for me to reflect upon what God has done for me and for us – hence the symbolic use of the Jordan crossing in terms of Christian baptism. This concern, of what God has done 'for me' reflects the culmination of the psalm, the climax and goal of the language of the 'deeds of the Lord'. In other words, the language of the deeds of the Lord is not 'unhistorical', in that the language *is* used in the context of God acting in history – but in my (or our) history in particular. But it *need not* be historical in the sense that it refers to particular actual events in the past. The 'events' narrated have simply become the traditional or confessional way of speaking about the action of God – which is real and powerful! These 'events' say something real and true about God and his relation to us, whether or not they report actual events as an eyewitness would have seen them. The events may be symbolic events in the narrative 'world of the text'. Or, as Abraham Heschel puts it in a different context,

> History, what happens here and now, is the decisive stage for God's manifestation. His glorious disclosure is not in a display of miracles, evoking fascination, but in establishing righteousness, evoking appreciation . . . The grandeur and majesty of God do not come to expression in the display of ultimate sovereignty and power, but rather in rendering righteousness and mercy. 'He exalts Himself to show mercy to you' (Isa. 30:18).[7]

So, particularly as various ancient 'conquest accounts' are laced with reports of divine intervention in ways similar to what we find in Joshua 10:12–14, we should not become obsessed, as some commentators have, with probing the relationship between God and the 'laws of nature' as is supposedly shown in texts like this. Rather, it seems better to respect the poetic and literary nature of such reports and consider how they function in the narrative world, and hence what this says (indirectly) about God and the nature of response to him in terms of righteousness and mercy. Such an approach is by no means to 'sell out' to a 'liberal' or 'anti-supernaturalist' bias, rather it is to take the Bible with full seriousness on its own terms, and not read it 'woodenly' with reference to our presuppositions of how we think it ought to speak. In other words, such an approach is in fact a refusal to 'buy in' to certain intellectual trends of modernity in particular that have little to do with true Christian faith.

## Conclusion

In conclusion then, Joshua, and the portrayal of genocide in the Old Testament looks rather different now, as perhaps does the way in which we need to view the Old Testament and its interpretation. This does require a difficult and even painful shift in perspective perhaps. But then rather than being a troublesome text of conquest Joshua emerges as a text that challenges the community of faith to respond wholeheartedly to God and to be willing to welcome those seemingly outside the community who display the 'signs of grace', perhaps signs that are shown in terms of justice, wisdom, love and goodness for example.[8] If one may speak of such a thing as the 'Joshua delusion' then perhaps it is reflected in Joshua 5:13 where Joshua himself assumes that God simply 'takes sides' defined by various ideologies and interests in the world. This 'delusion', or ideology or theology if you like, is corrected by the commander of the Lord's army who refuses Joshua's question, redirecting it to show Joshua that the correct kind of response to God is one of worship and faithful responsiveness that is developed in the stories that follow, stories that leave the limits of faithful response rather ill-defined even if its centre is clear, a centre that is now faithful acceptance of and loving response to Jesus embodied in terms of love of one's neighbour.

# Response to Douglas Earl

## Christopher J. H. Wright

This book by Douglas Earl is a stimulating and challenging contribution to how we think about the book of Joshua and there is much in his argument that is welcome and illuminating, as well as some points on which I still find myself uncomfortable and questioning. I think Earl goes a long way in enabling a different and more fruitful reading of the book, but does not quite manage to remove it from the category of being a 'troublesome text of conquest' (p. 138). This is an issue that I have wrestled with for many years as a teacher and preacher on the Old Testament. I make no claim to have 'solved' the ethical problems readers have always found in Joshua, but my own perspectives (for what they are worth) are offered in my own book, *The God I Don't Understand: Reflections on Tough Questions of Faith*.[1]

Let me begin with a list of points where I respond with grateful appreciation of Earl's contributions, before moving on to some more challenging questions.

1. It is certainly right to remind us that the book of Joshua is not 'just history' – any more than the four gospels are 'just biography'. Earl rightly pays attention to the literary form and theological intentions of the book and the overall message it is seeking to present, and does so in some creative new directions.

2. Earl is certainly right to point out the remarkable placing and significance of the story of Rahab. The first Canaanite we meet in the narrative is a converted one who gets saved. When set alongside the balancing story of Achan, an Israelite who steps outside the realm of covenantal obedience to God

and is destroyed, we are presented with a profound double paradox that is theologically subversive of any idea that Joshua is about a dominant or privileged ethnicity. Outsiders are brought in and insiders are expelled. What counts, therefore, as the challenging little episode in the middle (Josh 5:13–15) makes clear, is not which nation has God on its side, but what people are choosing to align themselves with the purpose of God.

3. Alongside this, I also agree with Earl's point that, just as the Rahab-Achan narratives subvert the assumption of privileged ethnicity, so chapter 22 subverts the assumption that land and geography are determinative of Israelite identity (p. 92).

4. Nevertheless, although ethnicity and land are not finally determinative, Earl is right to insist that a major part of the theological function of the book of Joshua is to shape Israel's self-understanding and identity in relationship to their God, and to illustrate the kind of demands that flow from that relationship.

5. Earl's discussion of *herem* is enlightening and valuable. As I will say below, I cannot avoid altogether the assumption that it included death and destruction to some degree, but it is certainly worth pondering Earl's presentation of its literary and theological functioning as a test of loyalty.

6. I agree that the book of Joshua must be read in the light of Deuteronomy, and especially Deuteronomy 7, though as I will expand below, I was struck by the absence of discussion of the relevance of Deuteronomy 9.

7. Finally, whatever our view of 'what actually happened' in the emergence of Israel on the land of Canaan, or our view of the historical nature (or otherwise) of the narratives in the book of Joshua, it is right to insist that the book describes a unique sequence of events and should not be used as a model or warrant for genocide or any other form of ethnic violence by Christians (as sadly it has been in the history of Christianity through the ages and in recent times). Part of our ethical discomfort with the book undoubtedly stems from that dreadful legacy of hermeneutical abuse.

Moving on to some areas where I remain troubled:

1. Earl attempts to reclaim the category of myth as used in a
   technical sense by anthropologists and others. I fully understand the difference between the popular use of the word
   'myth' (as meaning a story or a claim that may have a lot of
   popular belief but is fundamentally untrue), and its technical meaning as a story told within a culture to provide a
   sense of identity and meaning (which may or may not have
   elements of historical facts within it, but either way expresses 'truth' as perceived within that cultural worldview).
   Thus, we may choose in the latter sense to speak of the creation stories in Genesis as 'myth', meaning by that that they
   communicate the truth about creation within the biblical
   worldview even if their literary form includes poetic and
   figurative features.

However, the popular and negative sense of the word is so
ingrained now that it seems to me a confusing disservice to
our attempts to understand and communicate the richness of
the biblical text by using the word, while trying to salvage
some positive technical meaning for it that ordinary people
simply do not relate to. When politicians or commentators say
that some cherished view of things 'is a myth', they regularly
mean 'that's what we'd all like to believe but it just isn't so.' A
myth, as generally used today, means a popular idea that has
no basis at all in fact – i.e. a mistaken assumption at best, or a
malicious distortion at worst. I just don't think it is a word we
should go on using about the Bible at any level.

I was not greatly helped either by Earl's discussion of symbols and allegory and the difference between them. I do of
course accept that any (possibly all?) biblical narrative *points*
beyond itself (i.e. beyond the simple events that it narrates),
and that the literary skill of the biblical writers can generate
enormous symbolic power and theological resonance in the
way they structure their narratives. But there does seem to be
a difference between, on the one hand, narratives embedded in
books that purport to make some historical affirmation about
real people in the real world of the past who actually did

certain things and from whose actions a new historical situation arose, and narratives, on the other hand, that are intentionally constructed out of the imagination in order to make some point or ask some question (as in parables, whether of Nathan or Jesus).

So while I agree that Origen had a point when he said that the ethical and historical difficulties of some Old Testament texts, such as Joshua, force us to look for deeper significance – which he then went on to do in a spiritual and allegorical fashion – I am not convinced that Earl has avoided the main problem with such an approach, namely that it takes the whole thing out of the realm of real earthy history. Unless one is prepared to say that nothing remotely like what the book of Joshua describes actually happened at all (and Earl does not seem willing to go *that* far, though at the end of the book he remains agnostic), then to the extent that Israel's emergence on the soil of Canaan involved violence and destruction of *some* kind the ethical problem remains. Unless we take Joshua as entirely fictional, then it was not symbolic or allegorical Israelites who invaded (or settled, or revolted), and it was not symbolic or allegorical Canaanites who perished in the conflict.

2. This leads to my second major difficulty. In order to make his valid point that the book of Joshua has a theological agenda and is making a strong covenantal and ethical challenge to the people of Israel, and for that reason should not be construed merely as a 'history of the conquest', Earl repeatedly says that the book is 'not really a conquest account'. Now I agree that it is not a conquest account like the ones we have from other ancient peoples. I agree that it is not *merely* a conquest account, told for no other reason than to give us the facts. I agree that it is not a conquest account that glorifies the military exploits of the Israelites or the bloodshed of war. And of course, as I said above, I agree that the structuring of the internal narratives is highly theologically and ethically significant – even to the extent of undermining the kind of inferences that might be drawn from a shallow understanding of the conquest itself (e.g., ethnic pride, or divine favouritism).

However, I am not persuaded that the assumption of a historically factual basis underlying the book is irrelevant to the book's theological purpose, or that a concern to understand and affirm that underlying historical foundation is merely the product of modernity's historicist obsession. I think Earl too quickly dismisses historical interest in the book as a modern fad – the fruit of thinking that the only kind of 'truth' is what can be historically verified. Of course, I deplore just as much as he does the kind of scholarship and commentaries that devote all their energy to 'the world behind the text' in all its archaeological and critical detail, and say nothing at all about the literary and theological richness of 'the world in the text', and even less about the enormous challenge of the book to 'the world in front of the text' – starting with the Israelites who read it right down to our own contemporary reading. However, I cannot so easily relinquish the importance of a world behind the text that stands in some referential relationship to what the book narrates.

Thus, for example, while I value the importance Earl gives to the balancing stories of Rahab and Achan, I struggle to agree that the intervening story of Jericho is merely a narrative feature which is there to make the wider story 'work'. I dislike 'slippery slope' arguments, but is there not a real one here? If stories could be entirely invented merely in order to serve a literary-theological purpose, where do we stop in detecting such fictions, however well-motivated? This is a question that applies not only to the book of Joshua of course, but to wider swathes of biblical narrative. A substantial part of the claim that biblical faith makes is that it is founded on events that really happened, in and through which the living God both made himself known and acted to accomplish salvation. That, of course, is what lies behind the famous declaration of Paul, with which Earl begins: 'If Christ has not been raised, your faith is futile.' Now I would not for a moment put every event described in the book of Joshua into the same category as the bodily resurrection of Christ. But I don't think the historical issue of the underlying 'facticity' of Israel's arrival in Canaan, corresponding in some way to the account we have in Joshua and Judges, can be waved aside, even though we recognize the importance of everything else the book of Joshua is aiming to say to its readers.

Earl uses an interesting analogy on page 123 – with the movie *Titanic*. He points out that the movie is not really *about* the ship's maiden voyage and tragic sinking, but is a fictional love story set in that context. Similarly, he suggests, the book of Joshua is not *about* genocide, but sets its narratives in the context of genocide in order to present its readers with major theological and ethical challenges. This is an interesting analogy, but it seems to fail at a key point (or to succeed, depending on one's view of the historicity of Joshua). For although the movie told a fictional narrative at one level the underlying narrative was entirely historical. There was a ship called Titanic, which did sink on its maiden voyage, with enormous loss of life. Earl seems to want to remain agnostic, however, about whether any historical facts underlie the book of Joshua. 'The story may or may not have strong links with actual historical events' (p. 128) – though he does not deny that Israel did engage in warfare and that this helped to shape her identity as a nation.

3. My third main question arises from Earl's use of Deuteronomy. I entirely agree with him that Joshua needs to be read in the light of Deuteronomy 7 – and indeed that there are interesting ways in which Joshua has somewhat subverted a superficial reading of the opening verses of that chapter. I appreciate the way Earl makes clear the *primary* challenge of both texts, which is for the people of God to be uncompromising in their loyalty to the living God and give no place to idolatry.

However, I found no adequate discussion in the book of the perspective on the conquest that we have in Deuteronomy 9. There, in a way that is similar to the subversion of ethnicity as a claim for divine favour in the story of Rahab in Joshua – only much more directly – we encounter a very strong subversion of the idea that Israel would drive out the Canaanite nations because of their own moral superiority. On the contrary, Israel deserved to be destroyed as much as the Canaanites, and owed their continued existence only to the intercession of

Moses and the forgiving grace of God. The key point, however, is that *the conquest of the Canaanites is emphatically and repeatedly explained in terms of God's judgment on their wickedness.* This is a perspective on the whole matter that Earl does not seem to include in his theological discussion, and yet, if Deuteronomy is so key to the theology of Joshua (as he rightly says), this must be important. For me, at any rate, it is one dimension of the biblical portrayal of this event that impacts the ethical objections to it. Here is how I express this in my book:

> The conquest is consistently and repeatedly set within the framework of God's international justice and punishment. I believe this makes a major difference to how we read and understand the whole story. It is repeatedly portrayed as God acting in judgment upon a wicked and degraded society and culture – as God would do again and again in Old Testament history, *including against Israel itself.* In that sense, although the story is unique and limited, it is also entirely in keeping with the way the rest of the Old Testament shows God using nations as the agents of his anger against collective human wickedness . . .
>
> [In addition to the warning and anticipation about Canaanite wickedness in Gen 15:16], the degraded character of Canaanite society and religion is more explicitly described in moral and social terms in Leviticus 18:24–25; 20:22–24 and in Deuteronomy 9:5; 12:29–31. It includes the sexual promiscuity and perversion particularly associated with fertility cults, and also the callousness of child-sacrifice. This is reinforced in the historical texts, with additional notes about social oppression and violence (1 Kgs 14:24; 21:26; 2 Kgs 16:3; 17:8; 21:2). Now if we take all these texts seriously as part of God's own explanation for the events that unfold in the book of Joshua, then we cannot avoid their implications. The conquest was not human genocide. It was divine judgment . . .
>
> The New Testament accepts the interpretation of the conquest that is so dominant in the Old – God's punishment of the wicked. Hebrews 11:31 describes the Canaanites as '*those who were disobedient*'. This implies that the Canaanites had been

morally aware of their sin but that they had chosen not to repent of it but to persist in it against the voice of their own consciences.

If we place the conquest of Canaan within the framework of punishment for wrongdoing, as the Bible clearly does, then it makes a categorical difference to the nature of the violence inflicted. It does not make it less violent. Nor does it suddenly become 'nice' or 'OK'. But it does make a difference. The consistent biblical affirmation that the conquest constituted an act of God's punishment on a wicked society, using Israel as the human agent, must be taken seriously (by those who wish to take the Bible's own testimony seriously), and not dismissed as self-serving disinfectant for the poison of Israel's own aggression. Punishment changes the moral context of violence. We can see this in other situations in life that involve violence at some level.

There is a huge moral difference between violence that is arbitrary or selfish, and violence that is inflicted under strict control within the moral framework of punishment. This is true in human society as much as in divine perspective. Whatever our personal codes of parental discipline, there is surely a moral difference between a smack administered as punishment for disobedience and vicious or random child abuse. Similarly, there is a moral difference between the enforced captivity of someone imprisoned as punishment under due process of law for a defined criminal offence and the captivity of someone kidnapped as a hostage for no offence whatsoever.

The use of violence within a framework of justice and punishment may be problematic, but it is not simply indistinguishable from the use of violence in wantonly selfish, arbitrary, and malevolent ways. The fact that the Bible insists repeatedly that the violence of the conquest was inflicted as an act of punishment on a whole society puts it in a moral framework that must be differentiated from random or ethno-centric genocide. It does not make it 'nice', but it does make it different.[2]

All I would add to that is a related concern that, if we seek to resolve the ethical problem of the conquest by somehow divorcing it from the will and action of God himself, or by

ignoring the biblical language of judgment and punishment
that is used to interpret it, we will end up having problems
also with other signal acts of God's judgment, including the
exile (Israel being 'destroyed and driven out' at the hands of
the Babylonians), and ultimately of course the final judgment
itself. Indeed, we will end up alleging moral difficulties with
the cross – as some now do. This is an issue I also seek to
address in a section of *The God I Don't Understand*.[3]

4. I am concerned that Earl seems to disconnect the question of
history, in the sense of events that actually happened, from
the question of 'salvation-history', which he regards more as
a theological construct arrived at much later in the process
of combining the different perspectives of Joshua and
Judges. Again, I have no problem with the idea that 'salvation-history' is, from one perspective, a matter of theological
'joining the dots' between different events and discerning
the hand of God within them, presumably under the leading of the Holy Spirit on a strong view of biblical inspiration
and canonicity. There is clearly a retrospective dimension to
that whole process.

However, I cannot accept the ambivalence in the sentence that
'Joshua understood "as history" *perhaps* represents an important building block of what might be termed "salvation history"' (p. 127, my italics). There is surely no 'perhaps' about it.
The conquest of Canaan, including the driving out of the
nations and the gift of the land is surely an *integral* part of the
overarching biblical narrative of the 'mighty acts of God'. It is
affirmed as such in the Old Testament, and never questioned
(in ethical or in historical aspects) in the New.

This also stands against the idea that the conquest was an
act of Joshua and the Israelites – on their own initiative –
which they *mistakenly* interpreted as a command of God and
an act of God. Earl does not take this way out of the ethical
problem, but he does sail dangerously close to it in arguing
that we cannot read the character of God off the surface of the
text (and I agree if that means that we end up with a violent
Old Testament God whom we abandon with relief now we are
New Testament believers). Rather, it seems to me that we

cannot avoid including this event – carefully understood in all the nuanced ways that Earl helpfully brings to our attention – within the total biblical portrayal of God's redemptive action in history. Again, if I may quote myself:

> God promised Abraham that he would give the land of Canaan to his descendants (Gen 15:16). So the conquest is linked to the Abrahamic covenant. God promised the Israelites in Egypt that he would not only rescue them out of that oppression, but also bring them into the land promised to Abraham (Ex 6:6–8). So the conquest is linked to the exodus redemption. God gave Israel promises and warnings about their future life in the land, depending on their response to his law (Deuteronomy). So the conquest is linked to the Sinai covenant . . . The book of Joshua finishes the story of the conquest by saying that it was Yahweh himself who had fought for the Israelites and given them the land (Josh 23:3–5, 9–10). Psalmists affirm that the conquest was not really the work of human hands at all, but the power of God (Pss 44:1–3; 47:1–4). Prophets saw the conquest as one of the great acts of God and used it to accuse Israel of ingratitude (e.g., Amos 2:9), or as a metaphor for wooing Israel back to a restored covenant relationship with God (e.g., Hos 2:14–15). And even in the New Testament both Stephen and Paul refer to the conquest simply as an act of God's sovereignty (Acts 7:45; 13:19) . . . So the conquest is placed firmly within the whole unfolding plan of God in the Bible . . . We cannot simply say that Moses and Joshua made a sincere but serious error of judgment – in thinking (wrongly) that the attack on Canaan was a matter of obedience to God's command, and then imagining that their success in the conquest was the victory of God himself. For if *they* were so misguided about it, then so were all the other Old Testament speakers and writers who describe it in the same way. You simply can't surgically remove the conquest alone from the great sweep of Bible history, saying that it was merely the bloody actions of deluded warriors, while leaving all the rest of the story intact within the sovereign will of God. At least, you can't if you treat the Bible seriously as a whole.[4]

# Response to
# Christopher J. H. Wright

## Douglas Earl

I would like to thank Dr Wright for his thoughtful and important comments on *The Joshua Delusion?* I am grateful for his appreciation in numerous areas, especially with reference to my reading of the text of the book of Joshua, and for opening up important debates on wider issues of history and morality.

My primary response to Wright is to note – a point surely of considerable significance – that he does not challenge my reading of the text of Joshua. Wright appears more concerned with the *implications* of my reading for how we understand Scripture. He seems primarily concerned with the theological significance of questions of history, and secondarily with the questions of morality that follow from this.

But does a 'history-like' narrative in Scripture have to be (in broad terms) historical in order to provide a trustworthy witness to God? Given that it is the *text* of Scripture that the church has received as a witness to God and to the life of faith, and not the *history behind the text*, I am not sure that a 'history-like' narrative does have to be historical, even in broad measure, to witness to God. There are certainly important and difficult issues here that I do not wish to minimize, and I think that there is an understandable anxiety behind the issue of how biblical narratives relate to 'history'. But perhaps this does largely reflect our wider modern philosophical context that influences our perception of Scripture, so maybe it is our perception of Scripture that needs 'conversion'. I would be worried about what I have suggested in *The Joshua Delusion?* if Wright could show where my reading of the text is faulty, my interpretation poor, or if he could provide a reading that is a more faithful one than mine in which it is shown that a historical account of conquest is important. But I do not think that this is what he has done.

Turning now to Wright's specific concerns:

1. Wright is unsure about my use of the term 'myth'. I agree entirely that this term is problematic, and for over two years I tried to find an alternative. But eventually I decided to use the label 'myth' so as to reflect the anthropological perspectives that I was using. Unfortunately we must use words whose meanings shift – perhaps 'spirituality' is a good example. But I would welcome any suggestions for a better term than 'myth'!

However, I am not sure that Wright's unease here is simply with the term used. I wonder if it is also with the concept. Wright wishes to read Joshua more as 'history' than I do. But I do not think that the text is trying to recount history. As far as Joshua is concerned it was 'symbolic or allegorical Canaanites who perished' but *in the text*, not (necessarily) in history. Although Wright is concerned that I 'take the whole thing out of the realm of real earthy history' here, I am not convinced that this is the case. I would claim that the text *is* in the 'realm of real earthy history', but in the sense of the history of the community in which the text was created and used rather than in terms of the events portrayed.

Wright also suggests that there is a difference between 'narratives embedded in books that purport to make some historical affirmation about real people in the real world of the past' and those 'intentionally constructed out of the imagination'. It seems to me that there are several problems here. First, *if* one allows this assumption that narratives must *either* fall in the category of 'historical affirmation' *or* 'imaginative construction', how would one know the difference in a text that is around 2500–3500 years old? It seems that Wright brings contemporary expectations of genre to the text. Secondly, there is, perhaps, a pejorative expectation in labelling a history-like narrative as 'constructed out of the imagination'. But why should this be? If we take the great prophetic narratives of the

Old Testament as reflecting 'inspired imagination', then could one not suggest that likewise Joshua reflects 'prophetic inspired imagination'? Indeed, as I discussed in the book, Paul Ricoeur has gone a long way to breaking down the pejorative account that is often given of the 'truth' of fictional 'history-like' narratives.[1] Finally, I do not think that this dichotomy of Wright's withstands close scrutiny, and again it is Ricoeur who has done much to argue against the existence of this pervasive dichotomy. But in addition to this general literary observation, it is worth noting that as we come to understand more about the processes that led to the production of the biblical texts in the form that we now have, we see that it is often impossible to isolate a 'historical core' to a narrative without doing violence to the theological witness of the text. Inspired theological interpretation, development and retelling through the ages and earlier possibly historical descriptions merge and play off each other to make up the stories that we now have. I take it that this was largely Karl Barth's point (see chapter 1).

Our expectations of genre are very powerful in influencing our interpretation. To take an example in art rather than literature, Pontormo's painting of *Pharaoh with his Butler and Baker* (ca. 1515) from the group Scenes from the Story of Joseph is, perhaps, disorientating and confusing initially. In what is apparently the same moment, the butler and the baker appear twice, each being represented at two moments in time against the same scene and background.[2] What appears to us as a 'snapshot' is actually more like a 'cartoon', but in a single frame. If there were two adjacent scenes with the same background with the butler and baker in different positions we would interpret the painting without difficulty, but as it is, it is confusing. This is precisely because it confounds our expectations of genre. I would suggest that the same is true of Joshua. Of course, an art scholar would have little difficulty here, but this is precisely because they would be familiar with the genre of paintings such as this.

So, the question is that of how we know how to assess the genre of the work. I would suggest that it is by internal clues in the work and through the tradition of interpretation that has been handed on to us. So, first, I have tried to show how there are indications in the text that suggest that Joshua is not to be read as a historical narrative, such as the location of Rahab's house in the wall that fell, and in the depiction of the conquest as complete or partial in different parts of the book (e.g., 10:40–42; 11:16–20: cf. 16:10; 17:12). Second, I have suggested that throughout most of the history of the church Joshua was not read 'as history' but in a symbolic (or allegorical) sense.

So the question of the nature and significance of a possible conquest of Canaan by Israel is another question, separate from that of the question of what the book of Joshua is about.

2. Wright's essential concern again seems to be that of the 'historically factual basis underlying the book'. But my argument is that this simply is not what Joshua is about. It is another concern, even if it is an important one, relating to the question of how we understand the nature of Scripture. I agree that the analogy with the film *Titanic* does not correspond at every point – but it was, I hope, sufficient for the particular point that I wished to make, namely, that you can have a story that is set in the context of certain actual events whose point and purpose has very little to do with the actual events. In other words, *even if* there was a conquest, Joshua might be making another point entirely. It is Joshua that witnesses to God and not a possible conquest of Canaan which would be open to various interpretations.

3. Regarding the relevance of Deuteronomy, Deuteronomy 9 is a rhetorically charged passage the prime concern of which is to portray Israel as being undeserving of what they are given (the land). Israel's inheritance is purely the result of God's grace and not her righteousness (9:4–5). And part of the rhetoric is indeed apologetic, justifying the gift of the land to Israel as owing to the extreme wickedness and immorality of the Canaanites. But the wider rhetorical concern of the chapter would suggest that 9:4–5 is to be interpreted cautiously with regard to the significance of the portrayal of the Canaanites, even if there is no doubt that the Israelites perceived the Canaanites as a wicked and dangerous lot, perhaps with a good deal of stereotyping being

employed in their depiction in the Bible. Comparable in our time might be the portrayal of Nazi Germany in the twentieth century, or forms of fundamentalist Islam in the twenty-first. I agree that the Bible encouraged the revulsion of evil and wicked practices, and symbolized wicked practice in the Canaanites much as we would use Nazis or Al-Qaeda and their practices to symbolize the essence of evil today. I agree that God condemns and judges such evil, both then and now. However, *in Joshua* the parade example of judgment is found in Achan's story, not stories about Canaanites. It is significant that Joshua does not quote Deuteronomy 9, allude to it, or make reference to Canaanite immorality. Joshua is deafeningly silent regarding this text. Inasmuch as Joshua does offer apologetic, it is in relation to Canaanite military aggression towards Israel rather than in relation to their sexual or cultic wickedness, immorality or idolatry *per se*. (There is also the single comment on the hardening of hearts in Josh 11:20, but this introduces yet another category.) I do not think that 'punishment' is really the issue here, and if my reading of Joshua is correct, it is irrelevant for understanding Joshua.

I take texts such as Hebrews 11:31 as rhetorical in nature, and therefore to be interpreted and used cautiously. To take another example in the book of Hebrews, I don't know any Christians who are willing to take Hebrews 6:4–6 in a straightforward and literal way. The most convincing readings of this text interpret it in terms of rhetoric, which is not to say that it is dismissed or explained away, but rather that its message cannot simply be read 'off the surface'. Indeed, Wright's comment on Hebrews 11:31 that 'the Canaanites had been morally aware of their sin but had chosen not to repent of it', and his more general point later that '[t]here is a huge moral difference between violence that is arbitrary or selfish, and violence that is inflicted under strict control within the moral framework of punishment' are problematic in that no attention is paid here to the specific nature of *herem*. If we understand *herem* in a 'literal' way, it involved the slaughter of men, women, children and livestock (Josh 6:21). But in what sense would a six-month old Canaanite baby, or indeed a donkey, have been 'morally aware of their sin' and slaughtered 'under strict control within the moral framework of punishment'? I think that the moral problem remains for a 'historical' reading of Joshua in a way that it does not if one reads Joshua 'as myth'. None of this is to say that God does not judge wickedness, but that God does not necessarily judge *here* and in *this* way in Joshua.

4. It is here that I think that Wright demonstrates that it is the actual anthropological concept of 'myth' and not just the term 'myth' that he finds problematic. He observes (correctly) that I argue that 'we cannot read the character of God off the surface of the text', which appears to be an assertion that worries him. But this idea, of not being able to simply read off the surface, is often central to understanding myth. For example, Sir Edmund Leach asks, in the context of a discussion of the book of Genesis, 'But if myths do not mean what they appear to mean, how do they come to mean anything at all? What is the nature of the esoteric mode of communication by which myth is felt to give "expression to unobservable realities"?'

Is this worrying or problematic for the Christian? Yes and no. It means that the Bible is a difficult book to read and use well – but why should this surprise us? It is a witness to the maker, sustainer, and redeemer of the universe after all! This certainly makes biblical interpretation uncomfortable and challenging, but so is the Christian life. Perhaps we need to 'crucify' our modern understanding of the nature of Scripture. Paul makes clear that there are particular giftings with regard to teaching (which I take to include biblical interpretation), e.g., 1 Corinthians 12:28–29; Ephesians 4:11, and perhaps this is something that we have not taken sufficiently seriously, by not always recognizing that the Bible is a difficult book to read well. Why should it surprise us that the Bible is difficult? A greater recognition of this difficulty would probably be of great pastoral benefit more generally.

In conclusion, I think that the important question that Wright highlights is that of how we are to understand the relationship between the Bible and the actual history of the real historical Israel, and in particular what implications this has for how and where (e.g., text as myth, or events as history, to put it all too crudely) we are to find a trustworthy witness to God. Wright takes it that there is much less difference between text and history than I do. I do not for a moment wish to deny that God acts in history – I take it that God acts in the universe and in the life of each believer in every moment, and in special, unique ways such as in the death and resurrection of Jesus. But I take it that God can imaginatively inspire a fictional narrative that witnesses to himself, and that God may be discerned in the text itself and in the life of the community that is shaped by the text as well as in specific events, such as the crucifixion.

It is the *text of Scripture* that the church receives as her witness to God, and *not the history of ancient Israel*. Of course, these are inter-related issues, but they are different in important ways. I am suggesting that we do not discover the enduring significance of Joshua, or its earthy reality, in affirming the historical referentiality of Joshua's narrative. Rather, we discover Joshua's enduring significance through careful interpretation of the message of the text, as worked out in the community of people that the text has helped to form in their love, knowledge of, and response to God through the ages. It is in this sense that Joshua is historical, and thus part of an 'earthy reality'.

So if my argument is successful in suggesting that we read Joshua (and Deuteronomy) most faithfully when we read them symbolically as being about something other than the actual conquest of Canaan, and that the witness to God is *here*, with Joshua being concerned with challenging complacency in the Israelite and encouraging a shocking openness to the Canaanite in certain circumstances, then Joshua communicates something rather different about God than if one seeks to find a witness to God in the details of wars and conquest. Joshua is not about war or conquest, or God encouraging it. Israel clearly fought wars; presumably some were 'just wars', and perhaps some were not. We simply do not know – and we do not know how Israel emerged in Canaan. Theories of conquest, peaceful infiltration, and peasant uprising against oppressive rulers have all been proposed by biblical scholars and archaeologists, and have their followers. Clearly, these different theories influence the way in which we see the 'just-ness' or otherwise of the emergence of Israel in Canaan in historical terms. But the history of Israel's warfare (as best as we can reconstruct it) is not our witness to God. Rather, it is the text of Scripture – a witness that is often surprising, difficult, and demanding, although always enriching to grapple with in shaping our life of faith together, and I thank Dr Wright for helping us to continue in this process.

# Endnotes

## Introduction

[1] The difficulty of using the term 'genocide' in relation to what we find in the Old Testament might be compared with the problems of using the term 'suicide' to attempt to describe the Japanese practice of *hara-kiri*. Whilst at one level what the two terms describe may look similar – that of killing oneself – but at another level they are very different, with *hara-kiri* being bound up with cultural practices of honour in a way that suicide, as understood in modern western society, is not. I shall use the term 'genocide', but the problems of its use here should be noted.

[2] In this book I adopt 'user friendly' rather than technically accurate transliterations of the Hebrew in order to make the book more accessible. Moreover, as is common in contemporary debate, for simplicity I shall refer to *herem* without distinguishing between the noun and the verb forms which have different forms and spellings in Hebrew.

[3] R. Dawkins, *The God Delusion* (London: Bantam Press, 2006): 247.

## 1. If Jericho was Razed, is our Faith in Vain?

[1] G.W. Ramsey, 'If Jericho was not Razed, is our Faith in Vain?' in *The Quest for the Historical Israel: Reconstructing Israel's Early History* (London: SCM, 1982): 107-24.

[2] K. Barth, *Church Dogmatics* (London: T&T Clark (15 vols), ET. 2004): III/I, 82.

[3] J.J. Bimson, *Redating the Exodus and Conquest* (Sheffield: The Almond Press, rev. ed. 1981); P. James *et al.*, *Centuries of Darkness*

(London: Pimlico, 1992). See also K.A. Kitchen, *On the Reliability of the Old Testament* (Grand Rapids: W.B. Eerdmans, 2003), 159-90 for a more recent attempt to argue for the historical value of Joshua.

4  Postcolonial (or post-colonial) studies is a recently emerging and rather diverse field. If one takes colonialism to mean 'the conquest and control of other people's land and goods' (A. Loomba, *Colonialism/Postcolonialism* (The New Critical Idiom; London: Routledge, 2nd ed. 2005), 8) then postcolonialism may be seen as trying to clarify, understand and critique these processes, especially from the perspective of the colonized, often as a reaction against colonialism. In the same way that certain forms of post-modernism can be characterized by a suspicion of claims to be able to tell 'the big story' the same can be said of postcolonialism's suspicion of 'colonizers' claiming to impose their 'big story' on others. See Loomba for discussion.

5  R.A. Warrior, 'Canaanites, Cowboys and Indians: Deliverance, Conquest, and Liberation Theology Today' in D. Jobling, *et al.* (eds.), *The Postmodern Bible Reader* (Oxford: Blackwell, 2001): 188-94, 191-93.

6  R. Dawkins, *The God Delusion* (London: Bantam Press, 2006): 247.

7  D. Mbuwayesango, 'Joshua' in D. Patte (ed), *Global Bible Commentary* (Nashville: Abingdon Press, 2004): 64-73, here p.69.

8  Warrior, 'Canaanites, Cowboys and Indians'.

9  R.H. Bainton, *Christian Attitudes to War and Peace: A Historical Survey and Critical Re-evaluation* (Nashville: Abingdon, 1960): 44-52.

10  Bainton, *Christian Attitudes*, 52.

11  M. Prior, *The Bible and Colonialism: A Moral Critique* (Sheffield: Sheffield Academic Press, 1997): 29-36.

12  Prior, *Bible and Colonialism*, 35.

13  J. Calvin, *Commentaries on the Book of Joshua* (Grand Rapids: W.B. Eerdmans, ET:1949): 157–58. Such apologetic, and similar apologetic is still common, appealing to the transcendence and 'rights' of God and/or the sinfulness of humanity. See for example L. Strobel, *The Case for Faith: A Journalist Investigates the Toughest Objections to Christianity* (Grand Rapids: Zondervan, 2000): 118-22. Whilst I do not dispute the transcendence and indeed 'mystery' of God, the question is where one should make appeal to these qualities of God and where one should not.

14  See my 'Joshua and the Crusades' (forthcoming) for a study of the source texts. Bainton does not cite original sources in his work – he simply assumes the link. The gospels seem to be employed

because the crusaders understood their actions not so much in terms of conquest, but of sacrificial love for their brethren in the Holy Land who were themselves suffering the results of conquest. The motivation of the crusaders, as they understood it, seems best understood in terms of self-denial and love.

15  For example, in *On First Principles* Origen suggests, 'But if in every detail of this outer covering, that is, the actual history, the sequence of the law had been preserved and its order maintained, we should have understood the scriptures in an unbroken course and should certainly not have believed that there was anything else buried within them beyond what was indicated at a first glance. Consequently the divine wisdom has arranged for certain stumbling-blocks and interruptions of the historical sense to be found therein, by inserting in the midst a number of impossibilities and incongruities, in order that the very interruption of the narrative might as it were present a barrier to the reader and lead him to refuse to proceed along the pathway of the ordinary meaning: and so, by shutting us out and debarring us from that, might recall us to the beginning of another way, and might thereby bring us, through the entrance of a narrow footpath, to a higher and loftier road and lay open the immense breadth of the divine wisdom.

And we must also know this, that because the aim of the Holy Spirit was chiefly to preserve the connexion of the spiritual meaning, both in the things that are yet to be done and in those which have already been accomplished, whenever he found that things which had been done in history could be harmonised with the spiritual meaning, he composed in a single narrative a texture comprising both kinds of meaning, always, however, concealing the secret sense more deeply. *But wherever the record of deeds that had been done could not be made to correspond with the sequence of the spiritual truths, he inserted occasionally some deeds of a less probable character or which could not have happened at all, and occasionally some which might have happened but in fact did not.* Sometimes he does this by a few words, which in their bodily sense do not appear capable of containing truth, and at other times by inserting a large number . . .

All this, as we have said, the Holy Spirit supervised, in order that in cases where that which appeared at the first glance could neither be true nor useful we should be led on to search for a truth deeper down and needing more careful examination, and should try to discover in the scriptures which we believe to be inspired by God a meaning worthy of God . . .

> *And so it happens that even in them the Spirit has mingled not a few things by which the historical order of the narrative is interrupted and broken, with the object of turning and calling the attention of the reader, by the impossibility of the literal sense, to an examination of the inner meaning.' (On First Principles, Latin Text, IV.ii.9, in G.W. Butterworth (trans.), Origen: On First Principles* (Gloucester: Peter Smith, 1973), 285-87, emphasis added.)

[16] *Hom. Josh.* 12.3, in B.J. Bruce (trans.), Origen, *Homilies on Joshua* (FC 105; Washington: The Catholic University of America Press, 2002): 123-24. Note that the names 'Joshua' and 'Jesus' are identical in Greek.

[17] II.100, in E. Ferguson & A.J. Malherbe (trans.), Gregory of Nyssa, *The Life of Moses* (The Classics of Western Spirituality) (New York: Paulist Press, 1978): 77.

[18] Again, see my 'Joshua and the Crusades' (forthcoming).

[19] Although at this stage in the history of the Church the canon of Scripture had not been fixed.

[20] See e.g. *Adv. Haer.* 1.8.1 and 3.2-4.

[21] Or, at least, it is not being read as *Christian scripture*.

[22] For an evocative account of the moral problem of genocide in relation to Scripture see R. Rauser, 'Let Nothing that Breathes Remain Alive: On the Problem of Divinely Commanded Genocide', in *Philosophia Christi* 11.1 (2009): 27-41.

[23] For example, as in allegorical interpretations of the parable of the Good Samaritan, where it is common to find allegorical significance to every part of the story, such as where Paul is identified as the inn keeper.

## 2. On Wearing Good Glasses: The Importance of Interpretation

[1] For convenience of expression I shall speak of the Bible or of texts 'seeking' to shape identity even though one cannot really speak of a text as an intentional agent.

[2] R.A. Segal, *Myth: A Very Short Introduction* (Oxford: OUP, 2004): 56-57.

[3] W.G. Doty, *Mythography: The Study of Myths and Rituals* (Tuscaloosa: University of Alabama Press, 2nd ed. 2000): 33-34.

[4] See T.C. Butler, *Joshua* (WBC 7; Waco: Word Books, 1983): 21-22 on rest in the prophetic literature and L.D. Hawk, *Every Promise Fulfilled: Contesting Plots in Joshua* (Louisville: Westminster John Knox Press, 1991) on desire in Joshua, e.g. 37-40, 141.

⁵ The concept of symbol (and the related concept of metaphor) has been addressed in detail by Paul Ricoeur. In an important state-ment on the nature of symbol Ricoeur suggests that a symbol 'con-ceals in its aim a double intentionality. Take the "defiled," the "impure." This significant expression presents a first or literal intentionality that, like every significant expression, supposes the triumph of the conventional sign over the natural sign. Thus, the literal meaning of "defilement" is "stain," but this literal meaning is already a conventional sign; the words "stain," "unclean," etc., do not resemble the thing signified. But upon this first intention-ality there is erected a second intentionality which, through the physically "unclean", points to a certain situation of man in the sacred which is precisely that of being defiled, impure. The literal and manifest sense, then, points beyond itself to something that is *like* a stain or spot. Thus, contrary to perfectly transparent techni-cal signs, which say only what they want to say in positing that which they signify, symbolic signs are opaque, because the first, literal, obvious meaning itself points analogically to a second meaning which is not given otherwise than in it . . . This opacity constitutes the depth of the symbol, which, it will be said, is inex-haustible . . . I cannot objectify the analogical relation that connects the second meaning with the first. It is by living in the first mean-ing that I am led beyond it itself.' (P. Ricoeur, *The Symbolism of Evil* (Boston: Beacon Press, ET: 1969): 15.)

⁶ Hawk, *Every Promise*, 95.

⁷ Calvin, *Inst*. II.11.1 in F.L. Battles (trans.), *Calvin: Institutes of the Christian Religion* (The Library of Christian Classics 20; Philadel-phia: The Westminster Press, 2 vols., 1960): 450-51.

⁸ Doty, *Mythography*, 2.

⁹ See V. Turner, *From Ritual to Theatre: The Human Seriousness of Play* (New York: PAJ, 1982): 7-19, 122.

¹⁰ V. Turner, 'Myth and Symbol', in D.L. Sills (ed.), *International Encyclopedia of the Social Sciences* (Macmillan & The Free Press, 1968), 10.576-81, here 577. Italics mine.

¹¹ The account of neo-structuralism that follows is based upon S.D. Kunin, *We Think What We Eat: Neo-Structuralist Analysis of Israelite Food Rules and Other Cultural and Textual Practices* (JSOTSup 412; London: T&T Clark, 2004).

¹² See for example P. Ricoeur (ed. L.S. Mudge), *Essays on Biblical Interpretation* (London: SPCK, 1981).

¹³ Regarding the significance of 'discourse' Paul Ricoeur suggests, 'Discourse consists of the fact that someone says something to

someone about something. 'About something' is the inalienable referential function of discourse. Writing does not abolish it, but rather transforms it.' 'Naming God', in *Figuring the Sacred: Religion, Narrative and Imagination* (Minneapolis: Fortress Press, 1995): 217-35, here 220.

14   P. Ricoeur, 'The Narrative Function', in *Semeia* 13 (1978), 177-202: here 194-95.

15   W.T. Stevenson, 'History as Myth: Some Implications for History and Theology', in *Cross Currents* 20:1 (1970): 5-28, here 17-19.

16   See Ricoeur, *Essays*.

17   I discuss this in more detail in terms of 'cultural memory' in relation to Genesis 34 in 'Towards a Christian Hermeneutic of Old Testament Narrative: Why Genesis 34 fails to find Christian Significance' (forthcoming).

## 3. Clearing the Ground: Understanding Joshua as an Ancient Text

1   As I noted at the end of the last chapter, it is worth noting that in the Jewish canon (the 'Hebrew Bible'), of what we call the Old Testament, the books are ordered and grouped differently from what we have in our Old Testament. In our Bibles the way that Joshua is placed tends to invite one to read it as part of a big historical narrative. In the Hebrew Bible Joshua is classified and grouped with the 'prophets', which is suggestive of less of a focus on historical concerns.

2   Joshua 1–12 also reflects Numbers, but it is shaped most decisively by concerns from Deuteronomy.

3   But note that the so-called 'priestly' material (P), whilst most clearly manifested in the book of Leviticus, pervades the books of Genesis, Exodus and Numbers along with other ancient material traditionally termed 'Elohist' (E) or 'Yahwist' (J). The book of Deuteronomy is, as the name suggests, characterized by 'deuteronomistic' (D) material. In what follows I suggest that Joshua is composed of essentially a D section and a P section. Although the traditional division into J, E, D and P sources is now regarded as problematic by many scholars, the existence of D and P sources is not disputed, even though their date, extent and relationship is.

4   For simplicity I shall not differentiate between 'deuteronomic' and 'deuteronomistic' material. The former term refers specifically to

the book of Deuteronomy and the latter to the tradition that is understood to be influenced by Deuteronomy as expressed in the books of Joshua, Samuel and Kings.

5  See R.S. Hess, *Joshua* (Tyndale Old Testament Commentaries; Leicester: IVP, 1996): 247-49, 261.

6  K. Lawson Younger Jr., *Ancient Conquest Accounts: A Study in Ancient Near Eastern and Biblical History Writing* (JSOTSup 98; Sheffield: JSOT Press, 1990).

7  Aššur prism, III.7-31, in *Ancient Conquest Accounts*, 83–84.

8  From *MDOG* 115 (1983): 82–83, in *Ancient Conquest Accounts*, 210.

9  The Ugaritic text KTU 1.13, possibly the Sabean RES 3945 and, most importantly, the Moabite Mesha Inscription. See P.D. Stern, *The Biblical Herem: A Window on Israel's Religious Experience* (Brown Judaic Studies 211; Atlanta: Scholar's Press, 1991) and L.A.S. Monroe, 'Israelite, Moabite and Sabaean War-*herem* Traditions and the Forging of National Identity: Reconsidering the Sabean Text RES 3945 in Light of Biblical and Moabite Evidence', in *VT* 57 (2007): 318-41.

10  Translation: K.A.D. Smelik, 'The Inscription of King Mesha', in W.W. Hallo (ed), *The Context of Scripture Volume II: Monumental Inscriptions from the Biblical World* (Leiden: Brill, 2003): 137-38, emphasis added.

11  The issue here is the translation of the *lamed* preposition in Hebrew, a preposition that has a very wide range of meaning.

12  This understanding is common in the commentaries on Joshua. See J.S. Kaminsky, 'Joshua 7: A Reassessment of the Israelite Conceptions of Corporate Punishment', in S.W. Holloway and L.K. Handy (eds), *The Pitcher is Broken: Memorial Essays for Gösta W. Ahlström* (JSOTSup 190; Sheffield: Sheffield Academic Press, 1995): 315-46 for a detailed exposition of this view.

13  See Stern, *The Biblical Herem* for this idea, an idea that I develop in *Reading Joshua as Christian Scripture*.

14  This sort of association is also suggested in the Mesha Inscription, as can be seen above. However, it would seem that the concept of *herem* as found in Deuteronomy 7 in particular is rather narrow and specific in the same way that the concept of *herem* as found in Leviticus 27 is narrow and specific in a different way. Perhaps then the deuteronomistic and priestly concepts of *herem* in the Old Testament represent the isolation and development of different aspects of *herem* in the wider ancient Near Eastern context, such as is found in the Mesha Inscription.

## 4. Reading Joshua

1   See F.A. Spina, *The Faith of the Outsider: Exclusion and Inclusion in the Biblical Story* (Grand Rapids: W.B. Eerdmans, 2005): 52-71 for discussion of the significance of the portrayal of Rahab (and Achan).

2   R.G. Boling and G.E. Wright, *Joshua: A New Translation with Introduction and Commentary* (AB 6; New York: Doubleday & Co., 1982): 168-69.

3   Cf. R.D. Nelson, *Joshua* (OTL; Louisville: Westminster John Knox Press, 1997): 59; D. Jobling, '"The Jordan as a Boundary": Transjordan in Israel's Ideological Geography', in *The Sense of Biblical Narrative: Structural Analyses in the Hebrew Bible II* (JSOTSup 39; Sheffield: JSOT Press, 1986): 88-134, here 125-26.

4   Nelson, *Joshua*, 59-60.

5   W.H. Brownlee, 'The Ceremony of Crossing the Jordan in the Annual Covenanting at Qumran', in W.C. Delsman, *et al.* (eds.), *Von Kanaan bis Kerala: Festschrift für Prof. Mag. J.P.M. van der Ploeg O.P. zur Vollendung des siebzigsten Lebensjahres am 4. Juli 1979* (Verlag Butzon & Bercker, 1982): 295-302, here 297-98.

6   Brownlee, 'Ceremony of Crossing', 300.

7   If one compares the Greek and Hebrew textual witnesses here, there are some questions relating to the circumcision of those in the wilderness. Here I merely wish to note that circumcision is constitutive of Israel's identity.

8   For the importance of eating food in the land see E.F. Davis, *Scripture, Culture, and Agriculture: An Agrarian Reading of the Bible* (Cambridge: CUP, 2009).

9   This suggests that the Christian significance of Deuteronomy 7 will be rather complex – on the one hand Deuteronomy 7 is one of the strongest statements of the rejection of idolatry, but on the other hand it is ethically problematic and qualified here in Joshua. I explore these issues in more detail in 'The Christian Significance of Deuteronomy 7', in *JTI* 3.1 (2009): 41-62.

10  So we see here that the question of when it is or is not appropriate to read stories from new perspectives is one of discernment based on a number of factors. Here, the use of *maal* invites a general kind of priestly perspective for the story overall whilst the very specific and different uses of *herem* in the priestly and deuteronomistic traditions suggests avoiding attempting to read priestly ideas of herem into the story here.

11  J. Milgrom, 'Priestly ("P") Source' in D.N Freedman (ed.), *The Anchor Bible Dictionary* (New York: Doubleday, 1992, 6 vols.) 5.454-61.

¹² See William Beeman's discussion of *zerængi* in Iran in which he discusses a number of stories that have resonances with the kind of behaviour exhibited by the Gibeonites in which the action was seen in positive terms (*Language, Status, and Power in Iran* (Bloomington: Indiana UP, 1986): 27-32.)

¹³ See W. Brueggemann, *Divine Presence Amid Violence: Contextualiz-ing the Book of Joshua* (Eugene: Cascade Books/Milton Keynes: Paternoster, 2009). Brueggemann offers a thoughtful reflection on the significance of horses and chariots in the narrative, and discusses the question of response to aggressive power bases in Joshua 11.

¹⁴ On the Anakim Mattingly comments, 'In the Egyptian Execration Texts (*ANET*, 328-29), there are references to several princes with Semitic names who are identified as rulers of *Iy-'anaq*. Many scholars regard this as a tribal name related to the Anakim, but this connection is not certain (cf. Albright 1928). Apart from these texts, which date to the 19–18th centuries BC, there are no other extrabiblical references that shed light on the Anakim.' (G.L. Mattingly, 'Anak', in *Anchor Bible Dictionary*, 1.222); The Rephaim, whilst not a historical people, are attested to in various Ugaritic texts. Their identity has been difficult to determine, but following the publication of *KTU* 1.161 (=RS 34.126) and its analysis by B.A. Levine & J-M. De Tarragon ('Dead Kings and Rephaim: The Patrons of the Ugaritic Dynasty', in *JAOS* 104/4 (1984), 649–59) it appears that they are to be understood as 'long departed kings (and heroes) who dwell in the netherworld' (656); The Nephilim of Genesis 6 have been compared with the *apkallu*, the semi-divine 'sages of old' in the Mesopotamian king and sage lists. They are understood to have brought civilization to humanity, but some are reported to be evil (cf. the sages (*ummiānu*) of the *Epic of Erra* I.147-53 (AD Kilmer, 'The Mesopotamian Counterparts of the Biblical Nephilim', in E.W Conrad & E.G. Newing (eds) *Perspectives on Language and Text* (Winona Lake: Eisenbrauns, 1987): 39-44); For the Amorites see G.E. Mendenhall, 'Amorites', in *Anchor Bible Dictionary*, 1.199-202. Finally, see B.A. Levine, *Numbers 1–20* (AB 4A; New York: Doubleday, 1993): 378-79 for a discussion of the entrance of these characters into the Old Testament.

¹⁵ See the commentaries of Nelson and Hess for discussion of the boundary lists.

¹⁶ The description is an idiomatic phrase from *mala* and *ahar*.

¹⁷ The Kenizzites, the descendents of Kenaz, are associated with the Edomites (e.g. Gen. 36:11) and so the reference to Caleb as a Kenizzite here points to his questionable origins.

18  Here, I follow Mosca in taking the text as referring to Achsah making a request of Caleb in 15:18 (P.G. Mosca, 'Who Seduced Whom?
A Note on Joshua 15:18//Judges 1:14', in *CBQ* 46 (1984): 18-22).
But I understand Achsah's action more positively than Mosca
does. Achsah receives a blessing from Caleb, amid abundant
blessings, with her action construed along similar lines to Rahab's
and the Gibeonites.

19  See Z. Ben-Barak, 'Inheritance by Daughters in the Ancient Near
East', *JSS* 25 (1980): 22-33.

20  It is worth noting that the Hebrew word *arets* lies behind both
'earth', as in 'the whole earth', and 'land', as in 'Promised Land',
and there is often some ambiguity inherent in its usage.

21  See L.D. Hawk, *Joshua* (Berit Olam; Collegeville: The Liturgical
Press, 2000): 227-45 and R. Polzin., *Moses and the Deuteronomist: A
Literary Study of the Deuteronomistic History* (New York: Seabury
Press, 1980): 134-41 for detailed analysis of Joshua 22 upon which
the following is based.

22  However, the motivation for the separation of Israel from non-
Israel may differ – Deuteronomy is more concerned with the prob-
lem of idolatry whilst Ezra is more concerned with the problem of
Israel 'mingling', a more priestly sort of concern.

## 5. Reading Joshua as Christian Scripture

1  See S.M. Schneiders, *The Revelatory Text: Interpreting the New
Testament as Sacred Scripture* (Collegeville: The Liturgical Press,
2nd ed. 1999): 175-76.

2  See http://www.telegraph.co.uk/finance/financetopics/finan-
cialcrisis/4142088/Iceland-to-sue-the-UK-over-anti-terror-legisla-
tion.html accessed 20th February 2009.

3  This is not to suggest that tradition, in particular, ought to provide
a straightjacket for interpretation, or that it guarantees good interpretation. Rather, the tradition of the Christian use of a text
provides pointers that indicate in general terms what good interpretation might look like, and how a particular text has been used
to form the Christian community.

4  This is to present a somewhat idealized picture in which the reception and use of a text is understood to reflect the drawing out of
certain features of the text in a way that is fitting with respect to
both the text and the tradition – i.e. where the reception and use of
the text reflects good reading and development of the text in new

contexts. In practice matters are often not so straightforward. For example, I argue elsewhere that the tendency to view Jacob in a positive light in traditional Christian readings of Genesis 34 provides a way of reading the text that is fitting with respect to the Christian tradition, but not with respect to the text as discourse ('Towards a Christian Hermeneutic of Old Testament Narrative: Why Genesis 34 fails to find Christian Significance' (forthcoming)). In this case, such traditional reading cannot be said to be a good reading of the text. In this case, if indeed the sense of the text as discourse is not fitting with the subsequent tradition, then perhaps one should not seek to 'use' the text, with the role of the text being understood instead in terms of 'cultural memory' (see 'Towards a Christian Hermeneutic'). In practice then the interpreter works within the tension generated by the sense of the text as discourse and the traditional development of the use of the text, a tension that is small and revelatory ideally, although sometimes it is large and problematic. I shall explore this tension with regard to Joshua in what follows.

5  I shall not develop this important and interesting question of the nature of faith in relation to Joshua – I deal with it in some detail in *Reading Joshua as Christian Scripture*, particularly in terms of an engagement with Aquinas and Wittgenstein.

6  The question of the applicability of the dietary laws in the Christian context is, however, subject to debate. But I hope that my general point is clear.

7  See my 'Towards a Christian Hermeneutic' on Genesis 34 in which I argue, roughly speaking, that the point of the story is to deny the possibility of 'conversion' of non-Israelites to Israel, evoking the disastrous consequences of the mingling of Israelites with non-Israelites. In neo-structuralist terms this denial of mediation and transformation is at odds with the Christian construction of identity, and so it is a narrative that does not 'fit' in the Christian context.

8  It is interesting that in the later Jewish reception of this text, his confession brings him a share in the world to come (see e.g. *Leviticus Rabbah* 9.1), unlike in the Christian reception of his story where this aspect is not considered.

9  *Hom. Josh.* 12.1, in B.J. Bruce (trans.), Origen, *Homilies on Joshua* (FC 105; Washington: The Catholic University of America Press, 2002): 120-21. See also Gregory of Nyssa, 'The Lord's Prayer', Sermon 1, in *St. Gregory of Nyssa: The Lord's Prayer, The Beatitudes* (trans. H.C. Graef) (ACW 18; New York: Paulist Press, 1954): 30-31, for a similar interpretative move.

[10] Calvin, *Institutes*, II.11.1 in F.L. Battles (trans.), *Calvin: Institutes of the Christian Religion* (The Library of Christian Classics 20; Philadelphia: The Westminster Press, 2 vols., 1960): 450-51.

[11] J. Daniélou, *From Glory to Glory: Texts from Gregory of Nyssa's mystical writings* (London: John Murray, ET:1962): 19-21.

[12] I deal with these questions in more detail in 'The Christian Significance of Deuteronomy 7', in *JTI* 3.1 (2009): 41-62.

[13] N. Lash, 'What Might Martyrdom Mean?', in *Theology on the Way to Emmaus* (London: SCM, 1986): 75-92, esp. 89-91.

[14] In *Reading Joshua as Christian Scripture* I explore the traditional Christian use of the idea of *virtue* in relation to Christian identity since both faith and love are drawn together in traditional Christian accounts of virtue, a resource that the contemporary church might beneficially recover.

[15] I suspect, however, that many postcolonialists would be unhappy to go all the way with seeing the sort of reading of Joshua that I am proposing as being helpful in the construction of an ideology, for I preserve the importance of conversion and the metanarrative of God as revealed in Christ.

[16] I am grateful to my colleagues in the Biblical Hermeneutics seminar at Spurgeon's College in 2003–2004 for this helpful analogy.

[17] See S.N. Gundry (ed), *Show Them No Mercy: 4 views on God and Canaanite Genocide* (Counterpoints; Grand Rapids: Zondervan, 2003) for exploration of some of these possibilities, or more recently, and in a wider context, see the collection of symposium essays, 'Did God Mandate Genocide' in *Philosophia Christi* 11.1 (2009).

[18] For an exploration of some of these concerns in relation to Joshua 11 see W. Brueggemann, *Divine Presence Amid Violence: Contextualizing the Book of Joshua* (Eugene: Cascade Books/Milton Keynes: Paternoster, 2009). Brueggemann offers a thoughtful reflection on the significance of horses and chariots in the narrative, and on the vital question of the context in which a story such as this is read. However, I think that the significance of Joshua 11 is somewhat different *in the context of Joshua as a whole* than that developed by Brueggemann.

[19] An interesting example that shows great sensitivity to the metaphorical and symbolic nature of such language is found in the treatment of Exodus 15:3, 'The Lord is a man of war; the Lord is his name' in the ancient Jewish *Shirata IV* of the *Mekhilta according to Rabbi Ishmael* (J. Neusner, *Mekhilta according to Rabbi Ishmael: An Analytic Translation* (Brown Judaica Studies 148; Atalanta: Scholars Press, 1988), vol. 1. The translations here are Neusner's.)

Here, a number of scriptural texts that offer different metaphorical descriptions of Yahweh as a warrior are discussed whilst considering various human parallels for understanding what a 'man of war' is like. But the repeated refrain, 'But the One who spoke and brought the world into being is not that way' demonstrates a sensitivity to the nature of metaphor and religious language – God is *not like* human pictures of a 'man of war', although in another sense 'he is'. This is precisely how symbol and metaphor work – as something that 'is' and 'is not', but opens up the possibilities of new ways of thinking and feeling about something difficult to apprehend.

## 6. So What?

[1] See my 'Towards a Christian Hermeneutic of Old Testament Narrative: Why Genesis 34 fails to find Christian Significance' (forthcoming)
[2] In other words, this is not to say that Paul's letters, for example, are not to be read according to their 'plain sense'. What I am urging is that different parts of the Bible have different characters and need to be interpreted in different ways.
[3] R. Dawkins, *The God Delusion* (London: Bantam Press, 2006): 249.
[4] I think that Western society has been influenced beneficially by Scripture far more than many realize or grant.
[5] As regards history, myths in general may or may not relate actual historical events. For instance, one can happily join C.S. Lewis in regarding the gospels as myth whilst at the same time viewing them as reporting the death and resurrection of Jesus as actual events that took place in history. I am not, therefore, saying that 'history does not matter' as regards the Bible but rather that the questions of when it matters and the way in which it matters are much more difficult to answer than is often assumed. The importance of 'history' needs to be considered on a 'case by case' basis. Likewise myths may or may not narrate behaviour and actions that should form the basis for ethical models of behaviour, at least not when read 'at face value'. Again, the question of when narratives may be read at 'face value' as a basis for Christian ethics is a question that needs to be addressed on a 'case by case' basis. For the details of an ethical-theological argument against taking the *herem* commands literally see R. Rauser, 'Let Nothing that Breathes Remain Alive: On the Problem of Divinely Commanded Genocide', in *Philosophia Christi* 11.1 (2009): 27-41.

⁶ See M. Weinfeld, *The Promise of the Land: The Inheritance of the Land of Canaan by the Israelites* (Berkeley: University of California Press, 1993): 99-120 for discussion of various views of the emergence of Israel in the land.

⁷ Abraham J. Heschel, *The Prophets* (New York: Harper and Row, 1962), 1.214.

⁸ Cf. here Ellen Charry's discussion of Augustine in *By the Renewing of your Minds: The Pastoral Function of Christian Doctrine* (Oxford: OUP, 1997): esp. 121, 133, 137.


## Response to Douglas Earl

¹ Christopher J.H. Wright, *The God I Don't Understand: Reflections on Tough Questions of Faith* (Grand rapids: Zondervan, 2008). See Part 2, 'What about the Canaanites?'

² Ibid., 92–94.

³ Ibid., Part 3, 'What About the Cross?'

4 Ibid., 83. In the chapters of this book devoted to the conquest of the Canaanites, I explore much more fully its connection to other parts of the wider biblical framework of God's salvation – including the central point of the cross itself.


## Response to Christopher J.H. Wright

¹ Paul Ricoeur, 'The Narrative Function,' *Semeia* 13 (1978), 177–202.

² See https://www,nationalgallery.org.uk/paintings/pontormo-pharoah-with-his-butler-and-baker accessed 18/05/2010.

³ E. Leach, 'Genesis as Myth' in *Genesis as Myth and Other Essays* (London: Jonathan Cape, 1969), 7–23, here 7. He then proceeds to answer this question in the essay.

# Bibliography

Bainton, R.H., Christian Attitudes to War and Peace: A Historical Survey and Critical Re-evaluation (Nashville: Abingdon, 1960).

Barth, K., Church Dogmatics (London: T&T Clark (15 vols), ET. 2004).

Beeman, W., Language, Status, and Power in Iran (Bloomington: Indiana UP, 1986).

Ben-Barak, Z., 'Inheritance by Daughters in the Ancient Near East', JSS 25 (1980): 22–33.

Bimson, J.J., Redating the Exodus and Conquest (Sheffield: The Almond Press, rev. ed. 1981).

Boling, R.G., and Wright, G.E., Joshua: A New Translation with Introduction and Commentary (AB 6; New York: Doubleday & Co., 1982).

Brownlee, W.H., 'The Ceremony of Crossing the Jordan in the Annual Covenanting at Qumran', in W.C. Delsman, et al. (eds.), Von Kanaan bis Kerala: Festschrift für Prof. Mag. J.P.M. van der Ploeg O.P. zur Vollendung des siebzigsten Lebensjahres am 4. Juli 1979 (Verlag Butzon & Bercker, 1982): 295-302.

Brueggemann, W., Divine Presence Amid Violence: Contextual-izing the Book of Joshua (Eugene: Cascade Books/Milton Keynes: Paternoster, 2009).

Butler, T.C., Joshua (WBC 7; Waco: Word Books, 1983).

Calvin, J., Commentaries on the Book of Joshua (Grand Rapids: W.B. Eerdmans, ET:1949).

_____, Calvin: Institutes of the Christian Religion (trans. F.L. Battles) (The Library of Christian Classics 20; Philadelphia: The Westminster Press, 2 vols., 1960).

Charry, E., By the Renewing of your Minds: The Pastoral Function of Christian Doctrine (Oxford: OUP, 1997).

*Bibliography*

Daniélou, J., From Glory to Glory: Texts from Gregory of Nyssa's mystical writings (London: John Murray, ET: 1962).

Davis, E.F., Scripture, Culture, and Agriculture: An Agrarian Reading of the Bible (Cambridge: CUP, 2009).

Dawkins, R., The God Delusion (London: Bantam Press, 2006).

Doty, W.G., Mythography: The Study of Myths and Rituals (Tuscaloosa: University of Alabama Press, 2nd ed. 2000).

Earl, D.S., 'The Christian Significance of Deuteronomy 7', in JTI 3.1 (2009): 41–62.

_____, Reading Joshua as Christian Scripture (Winona Lake: Eisenbrauns, forthcoming).

_____, 'Towards a Christian Hermeneutic of Old Testament Narrative: Why Genesis 34 fails to find Christian Significance' (forthcoming).

Gregory of Nyssa, 'The Lord's Prayer', Sermon 1, in St. Gregory of Nyssa: The Lord's Prayer, The Beatitudes (trans. H.C. Graef) (ACW 18; New York: Paulist Press, 1954).

_____, Gregory of Nyssa: The Life of Moses (trans. E. Ferguson & A.J. Malherbe) (The Classics of Western Spirituality; New York: Paulist Press, 1978).

Gundry, S.N., (ed), Show Them No Mercy: 4 views on God and Canaanite Genocide (Counterpoints; Grand Rapids: Zonder-van, 2003).

Hawk, L.D., Every Promise Fulfilled: Contesting Plots in Joshua (Louisville: Westminster John Knox Press, 1991).

_____, Joshua (Berit Olam; Collegeville: The Liturgical Press, 2000).

Heschel, A.J., The Prophets (New York: Harper and Row, 1962).

Hess, R.S., Joshua (Tyndale Old Testament Commentaries; Leicester: IVP, 1996).

James, P., et al., Centuries of Darkness (London: Pimlico, 1992).

Jobling, D., '"The Jordan as a Boundary": Transjordan in Israel's Ideological Geography', in The Sense of Biblical Narrative: Structural Analyses in the Hebrew Bible II (JSOTSup 39; Sheffield: JSOT Press, 1986): 88–134.

Kaminsky, J.S., 'Joshua 7: A Reassessment of the Israelite Conceptions of Corporate Punishment', in S.W. Holloway and L.K. Handy (eds), The Pitcher is Broken: Memorial Essays for Gösta W. Ahlström (JSOTSup 190; Sheffield: Sheffield Academic Press, 1995): 315–46.

Kilmer, A.D., 'The Mesopotamian Counterparts of the Biblical Nephilim', in E.W Conrad & E.G. Newing (eds) Perspectives on Language and Text (Winona Lake: Eisenbrauns, 1987): 39–44.

Kitchen, K.A., On the Reliability of the Old Testament (Grand Rapids: W.B. Eerdmans, 2003).

Kunin, S.D., We Think What We Eat: Neo-Structuralist Analysis of Israelite Food Rules and Other Cultural and Textual Practices (JSOTSup 412; London: T&T Clark, 2004).

Lash, N., 'What Might Martyrdom Mean?', in Theology on the Way to Emmaus (London: SCM, 1986): 75–92.

Lawson Younger Jr., K., Ancient Conquest Accounts: A Study in Ancient Near Eastern and Biblical History Writing (JSOTSup 98; Sheffield: JSOT Press, 1990).

Levine, B.A., Numbers 1–20 (AB 4A; New York: Doubleday, 1993).

Levine, B.A., & De Tarragon, J-M., 'Dead Kings and Rephaim: The Patrons of the Ugaritic Dynasty', in JAOS 104/4 (1984): 649–59.

Loomba, A., Colonialism/Postcolonialism (The New Critical Idiom; London: Routledge, 2nd ed. 2005).

Mattingly, G.L., 'Anak', in D.N. Freedman (ed.), The Anchor Bible Dictionary (New York: Doubleday, 1992, 6 vols.): 1.222.

Mbuwayesango, D., 'Joshua' in D. Patte (ed), Global Bible Commentary (Nashville: Abingdon Press, 2004): 64–73.

Mendenhall, G.E., 'Amorites', in D.N. Freedman (ed.), The Anchor Bible Dictionary (New York: Doubleday, 1992, 6 vols.): 1.199–202.

Milgrom, J., 'Priestly ("P") Source' in D.N. Freedman (ed.), The Anchor Bible Dictionary (New York: Doubleday, 1992, 6 vols.): 5.454–61.

Monroe, L.A.S., 'Israelite, Moabite and Sabaean War-herem Traditions and the Forging of National Identity: Recon-sidering the Sabean Text RES 3945 in Light of Biblical and Moabite Evidence', in VT 57 (2007): 318-41.

Mosca, P.G., 'Who Seduced Whom? A Note on Joshua 15:18//Judges 1:14', in CBQ 46 (1984): 18–22.

Nelson, R.D., Joshua (OTL; Louisville: Westminster John Knox Press, 1997).

Neusner, J., Mekhilta according to Rabbi Ishmael: An Analytic Translation (Brown Judaica Studies 148, Atalanta: Scholars Press, 1988).

Origen, On First Principles, Latin Text, IV.ii.9, in G.W. Butterworth (trans.), Origen: On First Principles (Gloucester: Peter Smith, 1973).

_____, Homilies on Joshua (trans. B.J. Bruce) (FC 105; Washington: The Catholic University of America Press, 2002).

Polzin, R., Moses and the Deuteronomist: A Literary Study of the Deuteronomistic History (New York: Seabury Press, 1980).

Prior, M., The Bible and Colonialism: A Moral Critique (Sheffield: Sheffield Academic Press, 1997).

Ramsey, G.W., 'If Jericho was not Razed, is our Faith in Vain?' in The Quest for the Historical Israel: Reconstructing Israel's Early History (London: SCM, 1982): 107–24.

Rauser, R., 'Let Nothing that Breathes Remain Alive: On the Problem of Divinely Commanded Genocide', in Philosophia Christi 11.1 (2009): 27–41.

Ricoeur, P., The Symbolism of Evil (Boston: Beacon Press, ET: 1969).

_____, 'The Narrative Function', in Semeia 13 (1978): 177–202.

_____, (ed. L.S. Mudge), Essays on Biblical Interpretation (London: SPCK, 1981).

_____, 'Naming God', in Figuring the Sacred: Religion, Narra–tive and Imagination (Minneapolis: Fortress Press, 1995): 217–35.

Schneiders, S.M., The Revelatory Text: Interpreting the New Testament as Sacred Scripture (Collegeville: The Liturgical Press, 2nd ed. 1999).

Segal, R.A., Myth: A Very Short Introduction (Oxford: OUP, 2004).

Spina, F.A., The Faith of the Outsider: Exclusion and Inclusion in the Biblical Story (Grand Rapids: W.B. Eerdmans, 2005).

Stern, P.D., The Biblical Herem: A Window on Israel's Religious Experience (Brown Judaic Studies 211; Atlanta: Scholar's Press, 1991).

Stevenson, W.T., 'History as Myth: Some Implications for History and Theology', in Cross Currents 20:1 (1970): 15–28.

Strobel, L., The Case for Faith: A Journalist Investigates the Toughest Objections to Christianity (Grand Rapids: Zonder-van, 2000).

Turner, V., 'Myth and Symbol', in D.L. Sills (ed.), International Encyclopedia of the Social Sciences (Macmillan & The Free Press, 1968): 10.576–81.

_____, From Ritual to Theatre: The Human Seriousness of Play (New York: PAJ, 1982).

Van Seter, J., The Biblical Saga of King David (Winona Lake: Eisenbrauns, 2009).

Warrior, R.A., 'Canaanites, Cowboys and Indians: Deliverance, Conquest, and Liberation Theology Today' in D. Jobling, et al. (eds.), The Postmodern Bible Reader (Oxford: Blackwell, 2001): 188–94.

Weinfeld, M., The Promise of the Land: The Inheritance of the Land of Canaan by the Israelites (Berkeley: University of California Press, 1993).